CON...
DG738.14.M2B...711
MACHIAVELLI

W9-ACO-365

3 4211 000023815

R. Lane

WITHDRAWN

DATE DUE			
AP2 1 '95			
NO 0 7 '96			

DEMCO 38-297

R

23

GROV... D.
NEW ...ON

FIRST PUBLISHED IN THIS EDITION 1961. ALL RIGHTS RESERVED.

Library of Congress Catalog Card Number: 61-11371

Evergreen Profile Books are published

in the United States by Grove Press, Inc.

64 University Place   New York 3, N. Y.

in Great Britain by Evergreen Books Ltd.

20 New Bond Street   London, W. 1

First published in France by Éditions du Seuil, Paris, as *Machiavel par lui-même*

MANUFACTURED BY MOUTON & CO., IN THE NETHERLANDS

Machiavelli
by Edmond Barincou

117345
G

Contents

VIEW IN PERSPECTIVE

For two centuries after his death in 1527, Machiavelli's memory was very rudely treated. Two words, both libelous, *Machiavellian* and *Machiavellism*, were given international currency. In the ensuing confusion he was identified with Cesare Borgia, "his loathsome hero." Every sort of criminal act was laid at his doorstep. Catherine de' Medici was said to have got the idea for the St. Bartholomew massacres from him. It was he who taught respect for religion to the new absolute monarchs, the better to cloak the gratification of their passions. He was behind the Anglican schism, too. And he "counseled his prince in treachery, tyranny, and atheism." For every Christina of Sweden, who recorded her admiration in marginal notes in his published books, how many hasty, careless readers! Corbinelli, the Jesuit; the unknown hand that removed his name from the title page of his book; the publisher in Venice who felt he must disguise that name in the form of an anagram. In England his first name became a synonym for the Devil: *Old Nick*. Meanwhile, in his own country, he was given a sort of canonization-in-reverse: *San Machiavelli* is the patron saint invoked by those who look after their own interests first. Jean-Jacques Rousseau and Giuseppe Baretti defended him with

arguments that were crushing (for him). Frederick the Great denounced him publicly and practiced him secretly. In Warsaw, Napoleon had only the highest praise for Machiavelli; on St. Helena, he took it all back. With the Italian Risorgimento, romantic writers outside Italy ardently threw themselves into the task of rehabilitating his reputation, while Italian patriots so far overshot the mark as to turn one who had long been known as "the Devil's majordomo" into a kind of messiah.

In view of all the serious scholarly attention paid Machiavelli during the late nineteenth and early twentieth centuries, it might have been hoped that the real Machiavelli had at last been restored. However, the deeper significance of his work has never been accurately assessed, and the blurred outlines of his portrait have remained suspect. Not until 1942, when Augustin Renaudet published his 170-page essay,[1] did anyone succeed in placing Machiavelli's life and works in their proper light. As a scholarly tour de force, Renaudet's essay ranks with Léon Brunschwicg's study of Pascal's *Pensées*. He has brought together an enormous corpus of scattered and seemingly unrelated documents, including many drafts and unfinished projects; he has regrouped them, classi-

[1] See bibliography.

Figure representing the city of Florence (fifteenth-century miniature)

fied them, thrown whatever light he could upon them. Each
reader may thus reconstruct his own apologia for the true
political faith, following one or the other of the programs
which Machiavelli at various times advanced. All that these
extremely dissimilar and sometimes contradictory maxims
for action consistently have in common is the goal of the
country's well-being (whether under a republican form of
government or not), and their principal instrument is "the
reason of state." Machiavelli never used that term, but he
invokes the concept again and again as a supreme law.

Leonardo da Vinci once wrote that the man who fixes
his gaze upon a star never looks back. Machiavelli rarely
contemplated the heavens, as we shall see, and never sought
to stand on a height. He was one to keep his feet on the
ground, look Fortune squarely in the eye, and not flinch
or give ground even when the going got rough. It was often
rough for Machiavelli, but he could turn a setback into a
new advance. Here we shall make no mention of the contra-
dictions, the hesitations, the indecisions which Renaudet
sometimes discerns in his abstract thought. Rather, we shall
trace Machiavelli's career on the plane of concrete history,
from first to last, recognizing with the Italian historian
Prezzolini that Machiavelli's life was itself "one of his
masterpieces."

Throughout his exemplary career – so strangely divided
into twenty-eight years of nearly total obscurity, fourteen
years of intense but unrewarded political action, fourteen
years of retirement that bore diverse fruits, and two years back
in the thick of politics – Machiavelli's fate was very closely
linked with that of Florence, in a period when the destiny
of Florence was no less closely linked with that of France
and the rest of Europe. A few dates will suffice to recall
this new chapter in world history, which opens with the
discovery of America and the first invasion of Italy by the
French and closes with the treaty of Cateau-Cambrésis in
1559, on the eve of France's religious wars. Our story
stops midway, with the capitulation of Florence to the forces
of the Emperor Charles V in 1530 – the posthumous de-
nouement of the drama of Machiavelli's life.

In his earliest writings, Machiavelli described how the
West was being pushed back behind its former boundaries
by the assaults of the Turks in the Adriatic. Noting these
last surges of the Islamic tide, he saw that Europe no longer

Henry VIII *Francis I* *Charles V* *Ferdinand II*

presented an unbroken front to the Infidel, that a Christendom which for seven hundred years had been closely knit in common belief was in his day being superseded by a multiplicity of nationalisms, some fully developed and some as yet incipient, but all much more preoccupied with their armed conflicts against each other than with the need to unite against Islam, their common foe. During his lifetime he was to witness struggles between the England of Henry VIII, the Spain of Ferdinand II, and the Holy Roman Empire of Maximilian I, and was later to witness the rivalry of Maximilian (and his successor, the Emperor Charles V) with Louis XII and Francis I of France. The prize they all sought was possession of the whole Italian peninsula, and to accomplish this end each of these great powers coveted the gold florins of Florence.

France at this time was being subjected to the joint pressures of Spain from the south and the Holy Roman Empire from the east. Rather than be driven back into the Atlantic, she sought to tighten her grip on the continent beyond the Alps, invading the territories of Savoy and Montferrat. In much the same way, Florence had been looking north toward France, her distant protector, when she was hard-pressed by greedy neighbors close at hand.

Italy in this period was to serve as the theater of a dozen wars and the prize at stake in all of them. But it was as yet no more than a geographical expression. As Machiavelli observed, it was robbed of the spiritual prestige it had enjoyed for centuries by a Papacy pursuing temporal power so desperately as to be "rushing headlong to its destruction – or its chastisement." At the same time, the existing political fragmentation robbed it of all conceivable practical power, leaving it a "tasty morsel," as Cesare Borgia put it, to be gobbled up by successive foreign invaders. The exclusive concern of the four or five largest Italian states was either self-defense or self-aggrandizement. Blinded by local issues, Italy was incapable of a broader patriotism.

Nowhere in Italy was this dog-eat-dog variety of internecine warfare more bitterly practiced than in Florence between the time of Dante and that of Machiavelli. Never for a moment did the horizons broaden into the perspective of a religious or national ideal. The so-called Florentine Republic did not even have the upper hand in Tuscany. Though she established a sort of Roman March along the Apennines to serve as a barrier against attack from the north by the Venetians, in every other part of Tuscany her claims to supremacy were constantly challenged by such lesser neighboring "republics" as Lucca, Pisa, and Siena. At home, Florence was no more able to hold on to her republican institutions than were her rivals; like them, she underwent the fatal metamorphosis of all muddle-headed democracies, and slowly drifted toward an absolute monarchy. For all her traditional fear and contempt of "tyranny," Florence unconsciously sought stability, a principle of order and authority, and all that was needed to make her "embrace servitude with open arms" was a little astuteness. The Medicis possessed more than a little of this, and the secret passed from father to son, as we can see if we read between the lines of Machiavelli's *History of Florence*. The Medicis' scheme for eliminating all competition was a masterpiece of cunning. The famous Pazzi conspiracy (a plot to overthrow the Medici dynasty) was anything but a spontaneous popular uprising, however. It was simply one of a great many similar instances of a power-struggle within the ruling class, in the long history of which the ultimate resource of democracy, civic virtue, was gradually exhausted.

This was the depressing political climate within which Machiavelli spent his early years. This was the knot he sought to disentangle, the puzzle he attempted to solve: from out of this confused and shifting chaos of historical circumstance he extracted the eternal guiding principles of history. This was the "matter" to which his mind gave timeless "form."

9

THE MACHIAVEGLI, CITIZENS OF FLORENCE

Machiavelli's two earliest private letters, dated December, 1497, are written in Latin and signed, in his own hand, *Maclavellorum familia Petrus Nicolaus*. All that we know of the history of the family leads us to believe that the "Machiavegli, citizens of Florence" had long claimed to be of noble lineage, and that the signer of the letters in question had been reduced to rather modest circumstances. Being nobles of Ghibelline persuasion, the Machiavegli had been obliged to leave their estates in the distant territory of Montespertoli at some date prior to 1293. They had then come to Florence, and built a house in the present-day Via Guicciardini, not far from the Ponte Vecchio. (This street was formerly a section of the old Via Romana, which ran along the left bank of the Arno – the Oltrarno – all the way to the south gate of the city, then known as the Porta San Meo or Gattolin.) As newcomers to Florence, they were obliged to trade their swords for the cloth-merchant's yardstick or the scrivener's pen, for to enjoy the rights of Florentine citizenship it was necessary to be a member of one of the city's guilds or *Arti*. Over the years, the Machiavegli family switched political allegiance from the Ghibellines to the Guelfs, the latter being a democratic party as

11

Bust of Niccolò Machiavelli (?) (fifteenth century)

mistrustful of the policy of the Church as of that of the Holy Roman Empire. The family produced a number of priors and more than twelve *gonfalonieri* (a civic office somewhat resembling the position of burgess in England). Among Machiavelli's ancestors we find one Alessandro, who died in the Holy Land and was beatified; there were also two fervent freedom fighters: Guido, whom the revolutionaries of 1378 listed as one of their *cavalieri*, and Girolamo, who died in prison around the year 1458 as a result of his opposition to Luca Pitti. (Their descendant, Niccolò, managed to make discreet mention of them in his *History of Florence*.)

The last of Machiavelli's *Private Letters* states that his death will leave his family "in direst poverty." We must avoid taking that sentence at face value. As Niccolò himself phrased it in the second of his *Private Letters*, the Machiavegli were "pygmies" by comparison with "giants" such as the Pazzi family (whom Machiavelli had attacked in his earliest extant *Private Letter*). Though there were others whose wealth and prestige placed them at the very top of the hierarchical heap, pygmy families such as the

Machiavegli were still comfortably well-off burghers as compared to the proletarians who made up the twelve minor
Arti. Besides a small private house in Florence, the family
owned a country place in San Casciano; Machiavelli's description of this estate in his will is as carefully detailed as
the inventory of a real-estate broker. When Alfred de
Musset was traveling in Tuscany, he paid a visit to Machiavelli's summer house at Sant' Andrea in Percussina, and
observed that the manor house was hardly distinguishable
from the tenant's farmhouse; he wrote that it had more the
smell of peasant quarters than of a country estate, and gave
off the fusty odor of a cellar rather than the scent of
lavender and rose-water. The minor gentry of San Casciano seem to have been closer to the *popolo magro* than to
the *popolo grasso.* In one of his sonnets Niccolò wrote:
"Land owners and tenant farmers eke out a living there,
surviving on nuts and figs, dried beans, maggoty jerked
meat, and dry bread whose only butter is the taste of the
knife . . . just enough to keep their beaks as sharp as wood-
cocks'." The reader, both of Machiavelli's private correspondence and of his official correspondence, will be struck
by the importance given to money matters. It was no small
undertaking, for example, to betake oneself to the "re-tailor"
(sic), Messer Guidotto, for the purchase of a ceremonial
outfit to wear in the presence of Cesare Borgia, so as not
to turn up booted and spurred in "horseman's" attire. And
the reader will not be surprised to find, in Machiavelli's
Art of War, an image drawn from everyday life: seeking to
explain the *battaglia,* a battle formation derived from the
Macedonian phalanx and the Swiss square, he compares it
to the way the staves of a barrel are put together.

It was into a family of notaries, intermarried with land-
owners, that Niccolò Machiavelli was born in 1469, the
latest of a long line of respectable burghers reduced to more
or less straitened circumstances. "On the fourth of the
aforesaid month [May] Niccolò Pietro Michel, [son] of
Messer Bernardo M. p[arish] of the Holy Trinity, was born
at 4 o'clock [in the morning] and was baptized on the
fourth." The sacristan of Santa Maria dei Fiori must have
been sleepy or hard of hearing when he wrote down Santa
Trinità instead of Santa Felicità, thus inflicting upon the
newborn baby the first of a number of misunderstandings,
not all of them so minor, which he would be obliged to

13

undergo in the course of his fifty-eight years, eight months, and nineteen days. As it was, he was registered as a citizen of the right bank of the Arno, rather than of that Oltrarno which may well have been the quarter of Florence closest to his heart. As we see in prints of this period, the Pitti Palace had not yet expanded to the dimensions we know today – three great six-sided structures piled one atop the other – and the unoccupied open spaces on the steep hill-sides up to the Porta San Giorgio had not yet been terraced and laid out into a public garden. Was Machiavelli remembering boyhood battles in this ideal wilderness when, in Chapter XLI of his *History of Florence,* he made it the scene of a strategic turning-point in the street-fighting of 1343 whereby the Florentine populace overcame their masters? Like much else about Machiavelli's childhood and adolescence, we cannot say. What little we do know, or can conjecture, is based on Messer Bernando's "Libro di Ricordi" – his memorandum book. In it we read such entries as the following:

Inasmuch as on the sixth of the same [month and year unknown], his [son] Niccolò has begun to take classes with Matteo, master of grammar, at this end of the Ponte San' Trinità, to learn to read his Donatello [a primer],

Death mask of Lorenzo the Magnificent

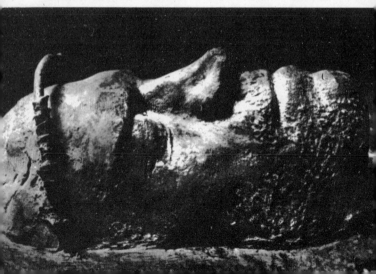

Bust of Machiavelli (?) (fifteenth century)

I am to give him 5 *soldi* a month, and the customary 20 at Easter. . . .

On the 5th of the present [month of] March 1477 my Niccolò began to attend the school of Ser B. da Poppi in the Church of San Benedetto dello Studio. : . .

On the 25th of the present month [June], 1479, Niccolò went up in the Mugello mountains to the place called Montebuiano to join Margherita and Totto . . . [he] brought me two saddlebags of hard chestnut-wood on one of Martino's mules. . . .

We shall not dwell on the extremely detailed accounts of the things they took along on such trips – blankets, black and yellow featherbeds, eiderdowns – but go on to note that Niccolò's childhood was not as "lonely" as Papini would have us believe. Between his mother and his two elder sisters, Primerana and Margherita, he must have received his share

15

Savonarola being burned at the stake (Anonymous) →

of love and attention. And doubtless it was his own father who taught him how to keep the Republic's records.

On June 29, 1486 (when he was 17), we hear of another kind of book – the book that his father, the notary, had him take to a binder in a neighboring parish to have bound "in half leather, with boards extending well beyond the pages and two clasps, for the price of 4 *lire* 5 *soldi*, part of payment to be in ruby wine at the agreed price of 50 *soldi* the

cask." This book was the first three *Decades* (*i.e.*, the first thirty chapters) of Livy's history of Rome, which twenty years later Niccolò would draw upon to create his masterpiece, the *Discorsi sopra la prima Deca di Tito Livio* (*Discourses on the First Decade of of Livy*).

He was a grown man by the time of the death of Lorenzo the Magnificent, an event to which he made one brief but suggestive reference in his *Istorie fiorentine* (*History of*

Florence): "A few days after the Prince's death in 1492, the doctor who had attended him was discovered drowned at the bottom of a well." Thus in his own lifetime he would have known about – if not actually seen – this ruler who rarely appeared in public during the latter years of his life, he would have breathed the well-disguised but oppressive air of tyranny that hung over Florence, and he would have assessed the price that the Florentines had had to pay for the peace that this prince had brought to Italy.

Two years later he was present when Charles VIII of France made his triumphal entry into Florence through the gate then called San Friano, passing through Machiavelli's own quarter, the Oltrarno, and Niccolò must have shared the mixed feelings of his fellow-citizens. The French were delivering them from the oppression of the Medici, it is true, but on their way to Florence the French had also delivered Pisa from the oppression of the Florentines. Pisa,

Con Gratie, & Priuilegi di . N . S . Clemente VII. & altri Prencipi , che intra il termine di . X .

Frontispiece of the 1531 edition of Machiavelli's Discourses a city over which Florence had had dominion for nearly a century, and which it was to take her fifteen years to reconquer! Piero de' Medici's tyranny, however ineffectual, gradually won out over Savonarola's theocratic ambitions, but his three years of excesses wore down both the rabid young partisans of the upper classes and the bulk of the responsible citizenry. Excommunicated by the Pope, Savonarola – *Il Frate* – merely thundered the louder. Rome called upon Florence to turn him over to the papal authorities; the Signoria was brought back into existence, and Savonarola's party excluded from representation. *Il Frate* began to get a tell-tale whiff of burning faggots and on the first Sunday of the Carnival season beat a strategic retreat from the cathedral of Santa Maria dei Fiori to his headquarters in the monastery church of San Marco. There he outdid himself in a rousing sermon calculated to make his withdrawal seem an adroit maneuver. To his misfortune, Machiavelli was among those present, and the third of his surviving *Private Letters* is nothing but a pitiless exposé of the orator's most elaborate sophisms as the miserable mouthings of a public figure whose career was in danger. The letter is our first evidence of Machiavelli's profound distrust of religion and men in holy orders.

THE SERVANT OF THE REPUBLIC

"I have neither slept nor gambled away these fifteen years that I have devoted to the service of the State. . . ."

It was shortly after Savonarola's death at the stake that Machiavelli made his first appearance on the public scene as a humble civil servant. On June 18, 1498, when he was one month past his twenty-ninth birthday, he was named to the post of secretary to the Second Chancery in Florence (an office which concerned itself with "internal affairs"). A month later he took on additional duties – without remuneration – as secretary to the Ten, a body which supervised affairs both of the Second and the First Chancery (the latter being the office concerned with "external affairs"). This little bourgeois republic was thus assured of a common link between various departments of government, and "Their Magnificences" – the members of the Signoria – had saved themselves an extra salary. Machiavelli was paid one hundred florins, from which ten per cent was withheld. We must not judge his employers too harshly: their economy drive was in part the price of past munificences, and what might seem to later eyes a certain confusion of powers

21

was in reality a healthy tendency toward centralization. Machiavelli never failed to stress the importance of uniting all the various functions of government under a single political command, and he was to help realize a further step in this direction a few years later. When that time came, unfortunately for him and for Florence, it was not one of Machiavelli's own candidates, the patrician Alamanno Salviati or Captain Giacomini, who assumed supreme command, but a succession of men such as Piero Soderini, of unhappy memory.

Machiavelli's political apprenticeship in the meantime was served partly at the Palazzo Vecchio, partly on missions outside Florence, either to other parts of Tuscany or "abroad" – that is, to courts of Italy not under Florentine rule. One of his first lessons in diplomacy (and one he long remembered) was learned in the Romagna during his first mission, lasting two weeks, to the court of Caterina Sforza – Countess of Forlì and Imola, granddaughter of Francesco Sforza, niece of Ludovico il Moro (whom she amusingly referred to as her *barba*), and the thrice-widowed mother of one of Machiavelli's favorite heroes, Giovanni delle Bande Nere, who at this time was a young child still known as Giovanni de' Medici. The "Lady of Forlì" was at the height of her fame, renowned as much for her beauty as for her romantic adventures; Biagio Buonaccorsi, Niccolò's faithful friend, once begged Machiavelli (in his *Private Letter 8*) for "a sketch of my lady Caterina's head, on parchment."

Her strategy with the young ambassador and Their Magnificences was decidedly feminine. After giving her solemn promise that she would "throw herself into their arms, setting all modesty aside," she took it all back next day, and when Machiavelli protested, she claimed to be astonished at his astonishment. She announced that she had slept on her decision, and added that "the more deeply we reflect upon events, the better we understand them." Confronted with such a right-about-face, Machiavelli admits that he was disconcerted and "unable to keep from showing his anger, both in his words and in his actions." His *amour-propre* as a young man and novice diplomat was wounded, and the mission was a failure besides. Florence was still faced with the difficult choice Machiavelli so lucidly described: On the eve of France's second invasion of Italy, with her support being sought by Louis XII on the one hand and by

22

Ludovico Il Moro on the other, she "could not make up her mind to side with either God or the Devil," and paid dearly for her indecision.

Thereafter Niccolò was never again to be seduced by the charms of great ladies. He was much more self-possessed in his later dealings with the Marquise of Mantua, Isabella d'Este, that especially touching Renaissance figure. Even with women such as the singer Barbera or the unknown lady of San Casciano – women whose charms he found irresistible, if we may believe his friend Vettori – it seems doubtful that he ever experienced real passion. The impression we get is rather of violent, short-lived bursts of affection, on no more exalted a plane than his amorous exploits with such women as Mariscotta of Faenza or Jehanne of Touraine. In this respect he was very much a man of his time, a contemporary of Ariosto, whose Orlando Furioso hardly strikes us as caring much more deeply about his Angelica than Machiavelli's Callimaco in *La Mandragola (The Mandrake Root)* cared about Lucrezia.

Immediately after this first experience with women, Machiavelli had his first experience with mercenaries – both leaders and troops – just outside the walls of Pisa. In August, 1499, the conflict between Louis XII of France and Ludovico Il Moro, the two princes between whom Florence still wavered, had reached a stage where the reconquest of Pisa, formerly a Florentine dependency, seemed feasible. Arms, men, and money were assembled and a brave *condottiere,* Paolo Vitelli, the master of Città di Castello in the Val di Chiana, was hired. In a solemn ceremony held in the Piazza della Signoria, Marcello Adriani, the head of the First Chancery, made a long speech in Latin and handed over the standard of supreme command. A council of war was held and Machiavelli's notes on what was said are as carefully detailed and show as keen a sense of strategy as his *Dell' Arte della Guerra (Art of War)* was to exhibit twenty years later. His clever scheme for capturing Pisa was not utilized until ten years later; when it was finally set in motion, its success was due to Machiavelli's planning and to the soldiers he had recruited and trained.

Meanwhile Paolo Vitelli and his brother Vitellozzo took the field so slowly and so half-heartedly that the repeated failure of their operations against Pisa alarmed Florence. The hired mercenaries were not keeping their part of the

23

bargain. Paolo was surprised in his tent, arrested, and dragged off to the Palazzo Vecchio forthwith. He was there put to the question, but nothing was got out of him: "They might as well have tried to torture a door." Somebody had to be the scapegoat, however, so they cut off Paolo's head. Justice was done so off-handedly that it is not surprising that the episode took on the proportions of the earlier scandal surrounding the execution of the Count of Carmagnola in Venice in 1432. The Signoria issued proclamation after proclamation blaming the deceased Paolo for everything that had gone wrong – as did Machiavelli in his *Private Letter 11* and in his later works. But public opinion was not satisfied, and fears mounted in Florence. Paolo's brother Vitellozzo had escaped the executioner's axe and was now an out-and-out enemy of the Republic, ready to conspire with all the other foes of Florence – the neighboring republics, the pretender Piero de' Medici, and behind all of them Cesare Borgia, Duke Valentine, who had the permission of both the Pope and the King of France to carve out a second dukedom for himself wherever he could beyond the borders of the Romagna.

The Signoria of Florence now abandoned its high-handed policy and sent one of the Soderini to Milan in the hope that the French might be induced to come to the rescue. The Governor of Milan, Cardinal Georges d'Amboise (who was usually referred to as "Rohan"), generously offered five hundred men-at-arms, but demanded that the foot-soldiers – numbering four thousand Swiss and two thousand Gascons – be paid twenty-four thousand ducats a month, plus equipment, rations, and an exorbitant bonus for breaking the pledge that his own King, Charles VIII, had made to Pisa!

After his encounter with the *condottieri,* Machiavelli now met foreign soldiers, and the latter experience was to end even more disastrously than the former. It began, in fact, with an episode that nearly cost the Florentine envoy to the Franco-Swiss army his life: When their rations and pay were not immediately forthcoming, three hundred enraged Swiss soldiers mutinied and, halberds in hand, attacked Luca degli Albizzi and took him prisoner. He escaped with his life only after the payment of a ransom of 100,000 ducats and the prompt intervention of Machiavelli on his behalf. But neither Florence, nor the Swiss, nor the Gascons, nor the King of France saved face completely. The Franco-Swiss

24

LVDOVICVS XII GAL

army fell ignominiously to pieces, and more than five months of negotiation were required to draw up even a rough inventory of the heavy losses incurred in the course of this ridiculous campaign. The episode does provide one noteworthy detail, however: The following year Machiavelli received from the Signoria the sum of ten ducats for his services!

The best men to send as envoys to the court of France to complain of this abandonment of the Florentine Republic in her hour of need were obviously Luca degli Albizzi and Machiavelli. But Luca declined so perilous an honor, and Machiavelli was appointed as negotiator-in-chief of the mission, his first to the court of France. Historians seeking to discover Machiavelli's first impressions of the affairs and people of France should consult the *28 Official Letters* he wrote during his stay at the French court.

Four years later, following a second mission to that country – which proved as arduous as the first – Machiavelli wrote the *De natura Gallorum (On the Characteristics of the French)*, an essay which seems to us to betray certain feelings of ill-will on his part. Caterina Sforza's abrupt about-face in 1499 had irritated him, and in 1500 and 1504 he found the vagaries of the French no less irritating. He later revised his opinions, however, and in his *Ritratti delle cose della Francia (Report on Affairs in France)* of 1508, and later in the famous confidential letters written after his fall from favor, he retouched this first portrait. Resisting his "tendency to base his judgments on his emotions," he eventually succeeded in forming his opinions "sensatamente" – on the basis of his own good sense alone. His views of the French are among the most penetrating ever written. They strike us as being the conclusions of a man whose personal inclinations, perhaps, led him to consider the vices of that nation as attractive as its virtues.

His admiration of Cesare Borgia, on the other hand, knew no bounds. For two years he both watched and fought this great warrior who was at once the open enemy of Florence and, in his eyes, the perfect model of the chief of state. Louis XII had given Cesare, already the master of the duchy of Valentinois, a free hand in the Romagna, and he thus acquired his second duchy. Cesare had then seized the chance to "rescue" the fiefs of Imola-Forlì, and next those of Faenza, from their more or less legitimate overlords, thus gaining possession of the main routes through northeast Tuscany. He then pushed on toward the Adriatic and wrested Rimini from the Malatesta, Pesaro from the Sforza, Camerino from the Varani, and Urbino – his third duchy – from Guidobaldo da Montefeltro, the latter having naively offered to lend him cannon for a campaign against the Varani. He then turned westward once again, driving Giovanni Bentivoglio from Bologna, the northern terminus of the "direct route" to Florence. The King of France was alerted just in time and stopped him. The King had realized what was at stake – but so had Cesare. Without asking leave of the Signoria – or making sure that he asked too late to receive an answer – Cesare crossed the Apennines by way of a surprise detour rather than by the direct route, violated the frontier, and crossed the territory of the defense-less Republic without striking a single blow. Setting up camp almost under the very walls of Florence, he now proceeded to wring every possible advantage from the situation; he even had the effrontery to offer Florence the protection of his arms and that of his captains – among them Vitellozzo Vitelli, the brother of the recently beheaded Paolo. Machiavelli carefully recorded, with cold and scorn-ful detachment, the cowardly capitulation of his fellow-citizens. Not only did they allow the promise of a *condotta* – which would have made Cesare the captain of Florence if it had been honored – to be wrung from them; worse still, instead of demanding the payment for damages that was rightfully theirs, they authorized the levy of a heavy tax for Cesare's war-chest and contributed a few pieces of artillery in the bargain. Let us note in passing that among the signers of the agreement we find the name of the future lifetime *gonfalonier* of Florence, Piero Soderini: the four-verse epitaph that Machiavelli wrote to assure the name of Soderini the most unflattering sort of immortality will thus come as no surprise to us later.

Machiavelli meanwhile followed Cesare's conquest of a State step by step. Since the King of France was barring his entry into Florence, Borgia for the time being was con-tent merely to occupy the approaches to the city to the southwest. After seizing Piombino and its roadstead, he also occupied the islands of Elba and Pianosa, and Pope Alexander immediately assumed the task of fortifying them.

At three points of the compass the maneuver to encircle Florence was thus well in hand.

Inside his own camp Machiavelli was busy observing – with equal admiration – and combatting – with equal tenacity – Cesare's effort to undermine Florence's strength from within, a campaign as cunning and effective as his attack on the city from without.

What was behind the disturbances that had begun in Pistoia in 1502 and had since continued without a single breathing spell? Seeking an answer to this question, Machiavelli had found it necessary to go to Pistoia in person, and with the aid of Niccolò Valori he had put an end to the uprisings once and for all by ordering a few timely hangings. In July, 1502, he had come to the conclusion that the same instigator was behind the rebellions that had broken out among the populace in the Val di Chiana, and demanded that they be punished in Roman fashion: their towns were to be razed, their lands devastated, and the inhabitants exiled. Let us not condemn this policy too hastily, in view of the fact that the occupation of the Val di Chiana would have left the last of the four points of the compass exposed, to the south of Florence, and would have constituted a veritable invasion highway, a route much more accessible to troops, pack animals, and artillery than the steep slopes of the Apennines on which the enemy cavalry would have found "nothing but stones for pasture."

The bitterest blow to fall on Florence was to come from the west, from Pisa – the conquered city that had rebelled, that ought in all right to have been retaken, re-subjugated, ten years before. Led by Oliverotto da Fermo, one of Cesare's most reprehensible henchmen, the indomitable Pisans had ventured outside the ramparts of their city and descended on Vico Pisano, a town more than four miles from Pisa and less than ten from Florence. (In the stark words of Landi, a chronicler of the time, the hapless townsmen, helplessly trapped, could "already see their guts in the ditches.") At this point the Duke, who plainly had the upper hand, "invited" Florence to keep the promises made by her *gonfalonier* and embark on a course that could lead only to her downfall. Seeking to refuse the invitation as politely as possible, she decided to dispatch her ablest spokesmen: Francesco Soderini (Piero's brother) and Machiavelli.

117345

This was the first of Machiavelli's two missions to the court of Cesare Borgia, and in the course of his duties he was to display the full measure of his skill as a diplomat. But the Prince laid down an ultimatum couched in such peremptory terms that Niccolò had no more than taken off his boots before he was again forced to leap into the saddle and gallop back across the Apennines to Florence, seeking something more substantial than "high-flown words" to placate Cesare. But he had had a chance to size up his outspoken adversary, and had found him a man much to his liking, both as a warrior and as a courtier. The warrior had earned himself a third duchy by means other than senseless bloodshed; as for the courtier, "one could not imagine anyone more splendid and magnificent."

In the first of the three *Official Letters* resulting from this mission we read:

> The victory of the Duke is due entirely to his knowledge of warfare: Having come within seven leagues of Camerino, he took time neither to eat nor to drink, but covered the distance of thirty-five miles, or thereabouts, to the gates of Cagli in one fell swoop, meanwhile leaving around Camerino a ring of troops who had been given orders to engage in skirmishes. Your Magnificences should take particular notice of this tactic, for together with great swiftness of movement, it led to most fortunate results.

In this instance Machiavelli (and Francesco Soderini, who signed this letter) should not be accused of applauding a dastardly deed merely because it was well-executed. In the eyes of the two Florentines this maneuver would take the despoiler to the other side of the Apennines, far from their Tyrrhenian coast. He would then doubtless proceed toward the Adriatic and descend on Venice, and to them Venice was an even more implacable enemy than a Pope's son, for Venetian mercenaries had invaded the rich province of Casentino not long before and had ravaged the countryside up to the very outskirts of Florence. Let us also take into account the fact that Machiavelli was doubtless taking a fairly wide view of the realities of his time. He was probably already engaged in drawing up his severe condemnation of Italian princes – both those who were legitimate sovereigns

29

and those who were more or less successfully entrenched usurpers. In the peroration of his *Art of War,* we will later hear Machiavelli's verdict, solemnly pronounced by Fabrizio Colonna, his spokesman. Let us also remark, finally, the note of enthusiasm displayed by Machiavelli in this passage. It is somewhat at odds with his usual sense of stylistic decorum, but it is altogether too rare an occurrence in his writings to pass unnoticed.

It was at this juncture that Cesare's star underwent its first eclipse: the duchy of Urbino slipped through his fingers; his ablest captain, Ramiro dell'Orco, was wounded; his troops suffered a crushing defeat at Fossombrone. The other *condottieri,* seeing the light at last, gathered at Magione, on the shores of Lake Trasimeno, to form an alliance against Cesare. All the members of this league were powerful nobles. They were also past masters of all the arts of skulduggery, and only the fear of a master more cunning still could ever have brought them together in one spot. The invitation extended Florence to join the league was tantamount to an invitation to step into a hornet's nest, however, for Louis XII had not yet broken with Cesare and had not yet withdrawn the hundred or so French lancers that he had lent Cesare at just the wrong moment. Once again Niccolò had to gallop off post-haste to the Duke's court; once again he was given the delicate mission of holding Cesare off, of putting him off the track with "high-flown words," thus giving the wheel of Fortune time for one more turn and the Signoria time to enlist on the winning side.

The entire responsibility for this second mission to the Borgia court fell on Machiavelli's shoulders, for Francesco Soderini was quite content to have escaped from the first mission with a whole skin. In the course of Machiavelli's first interviews with Cesare, the reader has a front-row seat at a comedy, as each of these two arch-hypocrites attempts to hoodwink the other. More than once, both parties conclude, amid bursts of laughter, that the match at hand has ended, fair and square, in a draw. But the moment for laughter soon passed when Machiavelli received definite instructions from home and was forced to announce that Florence wanted the Marquis of Mantuna, not Cesare, as her *condottiere*. Machiavelli's presence at the court of Imola was thereby rendered both useless and suspect, for a spectator as sharp-eyed as he might easily see through the clever trap that Cesare was carefully assembling, piece by piece, and expose it. His ambassadorial rank notwithstanding, Machiavelli was liable to disappear from the scene – with no questions asked – as suddenly as Cesare's own brother, the Duke of Gandia. The Duke, too, had stood in Cesare's way. . . .

For this very reason Machiavelli several times asked to be recalled to Florence, but Their Magnificences kept him at the Borgia court, by dint of entreaties and flattery at first, and then by a strict order signed by Soderini's own hand. His friend Biagio's requests that he return to the Palazzo Vecchio met with no success; letters from Marietta, his young wife, informing him that she had "lost her faith in God and was quite sure that only the Devil had profited from her dowry and her virginity and all the rest," were equally fruitless. No doubt it was Machiavelli's lively curiosity – and perhaps his penchant for the calculated risk as

31

well – that led him to choose, not too unwillingly, to stay and see the affair through to the end. In the course of these two months and five days – from October 5 to December 10, 1502 – he watched the Duke maneuver. Finding himself at the mercy of his sworn enemies in the beginning, Cesare soon got the upper hand: he simultaneously reorganized his army, so that this time he could be sure of its loyalties, and carried off a whole series of aggressive diplomatic moves. When Cesare finally left Imola and set up camp at the crossroads of Cesena, Machiavelli was faced with a grave problem. What would Cesare's next target be? Might it be Tuscany? – during one of their interviews Cesare had spoken of Lucca as a "tender morsel fit for a Cardinal." Or would he bow to the wishes of Vitellozzo Vitelli and Oliverotto da Fermo and march on Florence? Weighing the alternatives, Machiavelli wrote:

> But it has been snowing for four whole days without stopping, and no one has any desire to cross the Apennines. . . . According to some people here, he [Cesare] is bound for Ravenna or Cervia. The Venetians have a great fear of him. . . . The dignitaries of that city take the night watch themselves, as if the enemy were at the very gates.

On December 18, Machiavelli was obliged to send word to the Signoria that Cesare had again offered Florence his "services." Machiavelli faithfully reported that "it is doubtless a good thing that such services have been offered them [*i.e.*, the Signori], but it would be an even better thing if they were in a position to refuse the offer." Louis XII's unexpected withdrawal of his French lancers from Cesare's army had brought events to a head, and precipitated the choice of a theater of operations. The Duke now invited his new partners to join forces with him, and capture Sinigaglia, a little town on the shores of the Adriatic. They debated for a time, but were finally won over by the prospect of the rich booty that would be theirs. In the words of Machiavelli: "Their utter naiveté took them to Sinigaglia." In less than twenty-four hours the trap that Cesare had been carefully planning for three months was successfully sprung. Machiavelli dispatched to Florence a brief, anguished message describing the events that had taken place in Sinigaglia

32

Dapefalo ꝛꝺ

during the melodramatic coup: the sack of the city, to which the Duke himself had put an end, standing in the blood of his own soldiers; the arrest of four disloyal captains; the death of two of them, "this very night at the stroke of ten"; and lastly, Cesare's final, fateful ultimatum to the Signoria.

Machiavelli then joined the patrols out to track down the captains who had managed to escape Cesare's hangman, and again he witnessed events at first hand. Pandolfo Petrucci, the overlord of Siena, and Giampaolo Baglioni, the master of Perugia, had been clever enough to see which way the wind was blowing, and cleared out just before the patrols arrived in hot pursuit, abandoning their fiefs one after the other. As Cesare saw it, these estates now belonged to the Church – which meant, as Machiavelli saw it, that they now belonged to the Borgias. He also witnessed the fall of Perugia, in Umbria, and Siena, in Tuscany – two other supposedly impregnable fortresses.

The Duke then turned northward once again. But no sooner had he arrived at the Val di Chiana – where the road to Florence lay open before him – when there occurred another melodramatic turn of fortune. Cesare suddenly abandoned the road to certain victory and veered south. Had France intervened and vetoed his plans? Or was he taking advantage of a tactical error on the part of France and seeking a closer alliance with Spain? Whatever the explanation, Cesare hastened to Capua to join in the sacking of that city – a raid which saw Frederic of Aragon dispossessed of his estates by his uncle Ferdinand and Louis XII, his presumed ally by the terms of the treaty of Granada.

Florence heaved a sight of relief and promptly forgot the fate she had so narrowly escaped. And Machiavelli, after his name had turned up for "eight straight days" on the list of Florentines missing in action, was welcomed home by his family with open arms and by his fellow-citizens with respect. But unlike his fellow-Florentines he could not forget the events just past: though the sword of Damocles had not yet fallen, it hung suspended over the city still. His *Parole da dirle sopra la provisione del denaio (Remarks on the Urgent Need to Raise Funds)* therefore took on the character of a veritable Philippic to the Florentines, who unfortunately proved as deaf to his counsel as the Athenians had been to that of Demosthenes. Machiavelli had referred

to what rights the Florentines still enjoyed as "their petty freedoms"; yet they might have lost even these, had it not been for the lucky fact that an epidemic of malaria had broken out in Rome. It was malarial fever (and not poison, as legend would have it) that put the Borgia pope, Alexander VI, in his grave in August, 1503. It almost killed off Cesare, Alexander's son, as well, and the "hypothesis of the Prince" was therefore shelved.

The question of the papal succession having thus been opened, the Signoria again appointed Machiavelli – Florence's most loyal diplomat and sharpest pair of eyes – to represent the city at the papal conclave in Rome. In the accounts of this first official mission to the papal court (he was later to have another), we are struck by one curious fact: he seems to reveal his own thoughts only by what he does *not* report. We known that he was a fervent admirer of Ancient Rome, yet in all his forty-nine *Official Letters* he has nothing to say on this subject. Nor does he describe the Rome of his own day, though we know that several magnificent Renaissance palaces had already been built. But we must remember that Machiavelli could hardly have taken long leisurely walks through the city at this time: Rome was in the throes of an epidemic; the Tiber had overflowed its banks and even the Sant' Angelo bridge was awash; and walking abroad at night was worth one's life, for the streets were teeming with local cutthroats and hardbitten mercenaries brought to Rome by the Orsini, the Colonna, the Baglioni, and others of their stripe to help tip the balance of power during the election of the Sovereign Pontiff.

Let us regretfully accept the fact: Machiavelli's observations were confined strictly to the field of politics. He took careful notes, however, as the same old story of blackmail

35

and bribery repeated itself, and weighed the chances of the various papal candidates: the Cardinal d'Amboise, Francesco Soderini, Giuliano della Rovere (who at this date held only the relatively lowly office of cardinal of San Pietro in Vincoli). The outcome of the election came as no surprise to Machiavelli, the winner being the future Julius II, the *papabile* [papal candidate] who had paid the most and promised the most. Machiavelli immediately began to survey the situation and predict the possible repercussions of the election, devoting particular attention to the effect this event would have on Cesare Borgia – the prince whom he had most closely studied up to this point. But to our astonishment he now seems to lose interest in Cesare, who in his eyes was no longer the man he had once been, having been foolish enough to trust Julius II. Not to have known the value of a pope's word! Machiavelli also noticed that Cesare was losing the self-discipline that had so aroused his admiration earlier, for the Prince now fell into helpless fits of childish rage at the slightest provocation. Machiavelli therefore turned his attention elsewhere – or as he put it, let Cesare "slip into the grave."

Julius II, on the other hand, interested him more and more as time went by, and he soon discerned the new pope's strengths and weaknesses. By a brilliant stroke of cunning Machiavelli immediately began to exploit Julius II's hatred of the Republic of Venice, hoping to wring from him every possible advantage for Florence. (Following the death of Alexander VI, Venice had reoccupied all the estates that Cesare had seized; Julius, however, maintained that these fiefs were still the property of the Holy See.) In his usual fashion, Machiavelli cooly sized up his man, found the new pope a fascinating figure, and suspected that real courage lay concealed beneath Julius' apparent imprudence. His fascination was tempered, however, by his inherent mistrust of all ecclesiastics, a quality we have noticed before in Machiavelli.

Yet we are pleased to note that during this mission he reveals his own feelings much more openly, and criticizes others much less harshly, than he had in the sketches written in 1500. During this whole long mission in Rome, he was not only deeply interested in the events taking place; he was also deeply troubled, and carefully passed on to Florence the smallest bit of information that had trickled through to Rome from the frontiers of the Kingdom of Naples. For at this very moment France and Spain were encamped on the opposite shores of the Garagliano. Formerly allies, the two powers now confronted each other as enemies. But the two armies, with Bayard leading the French and Gonzalo the Spanish, had been held up for weeks on end by torrential rains, awaiting the hour when the great battle could at last be joined. All Europe was waiting with them, and for once Machiavelli allows us to see where his real loyalties lie.

Paola minora: the intimate little detail! From a brief letter from Madonna Marietta we learn that Machiavelli, when time and his diplomatic duties permitted, wrote his wife three letters – all of which were either lost or suppressed by his descendants. From her letter we learn that Marietta is concerned about her husband, as usual, and yearns for his return. She also writes that the *bambina* is sickly, but the new baby is "most handsome": his skin is "white as snow," he has lots of hair like his papa, and looks just like him. Let us note this small fact carefully: there are many different portraits of Machiavelli reproduced in this book, but this is the only authentic description of his physical appearance. It is confirmed by Machiavelli's friend Biagio, who in another letter writes that the baby has "hair as black as a crow." And finally, since History must not omit even the humblest detail, let us also mention the postscript of Marietta's letter, and awkward, misspelled scrawl that puzzled Machiavelli scholars for years, though its contents, once deciphered, proved as touching as its form!

Dame Fortune had spoken: the disaster of Garigliano, and subsequent defeats at Seminara and Cerignola, drove France from Southern Italy for all time, and allowed Spain to move in. Florence now lay helplessly exposed to the avarice of all comers. Her protector had been badly defeated, and was far off in Milan; the victorious Spanish troops were already marching through the Abruzzi toward Venice, having overrun Rome, which had not had time to organize an army. A second mission, with Machiavelli and Niccolò Valori as the two envoys, was sent from Florence to the court of France. To follow the events of this second mission is to come to appreciate the fine art of diplomacy. The real purpose of the two ambassadors was to drive a hard bargain with the King – if not, indeed, to blackmail him: the King was either to pay back the 10,000 ducats he owed the Florentines or they would, as Machiavelli put it, "seek salvation elsewhere." These terms, however, were so cleverly disguised as to appear to be nothing more than a respectful filial request for aid. The mission was a success, moreover, for the simple reason that neither Louis XII, nor Georges d'Amboise, nor Robertet, the Royal Chancellor, could discover the exact proportions of cynicism and sentiment that had entered into the compounding of Machiavelli's proposals – and the modern historian's guess is no better.

To return to humbler subjects, let us mention here one of Niccolò's legitimate sources of pride. In this third *Official Letter,* sent to the Signoria from Lyon, he writes: "I arrived here last Friday at about ten in the evening, and thus have kept the promise I made to arrive here in six days – or even less, if we subtract the time it took me to reach Milan." This was a distance of 192 miles. Machiavelli richly deserves the title Commynes gave Louis XI's first postillions: he is a "good galloper." If anyone interested in Machiavelli's life from day to day were to draw up a map of his travels by horseback – tracing only his journeys abroad, omitting the countless trips he made inside his own country, and making a rough estimate of the distances involved – he would find that Machiavelli covered well over 30,000 miles! This makes us realize how dreary the long years of exile, when he was forced to retire from active life and remain within the confines of his estate at San Casciano, must have seemed to him.

Our traveler finally returned to Florence, as happy to be back as he had been te leap in the saddle and gallop off. On February 25, 1504, he had written: "Since the day that the ratification of the truce with Spain arrived, I have been ready to put my foot in the stirrup and come home." He had made such a brilliant impression at the French court that he narrowly missed being sent back to Paris the following year, for Valori had been urgently requesting that the acting ambassador be replaced by "a man with brains, who does not stand on ceremony but gets things done." But Louis XII had broken most of his promises to Florence, and Machiavelli's intelligent, untiring services in the face of increasing perils – old and new – were sorely needed at home.

In his *Urgent Remarks on the Need to Raise Funds,* a speech that Machiavelli delivered to his fellow-citizens in March, 1504, we find these ringing words: ". . . go outside your own territory and take a look at your neighbors . . . two or three cities which would far rather see you die than live themselves." One of the cities referred to was Pisa; Florence was later to make a vain attempt to divert the waters of the Arno and drive the Pisans out of their city through thirst, having been unable to do so by force of arms. Another of the cities was Lucca, which had sneaked supplies in to the Pisans under the very noses of the Florentine troops besieging the city. He was also referring, finally, to Perugia and Siena, whose overlords (Giampaolo Baglioni and Pandolfo Petrucci) had escaped Cesare's trap at Sinigaglia and were lending secret support to a new adventurer hovering on the borders of Tuscany: Bartolommeo d'Alviano. Though the latter possessed only an insignificant little fief and was neither a pope's son nor a king's protégé, he was a valiant *condottiere* who had put up a gallant fight at the battle of Garigliano. Unlike Piero de' Medici, his comrade-in-arms, he had not stayed on at Garigliano, and the Franco-Spanish truce had put him out of a job. Florence had put Baglioni on her payroll and signed a treaty of friendship with Petrucci; still, either of the two might have hired d'Alviano. It was Machiavelli's task to dig out the truth of the matter and make them blush for shame – if such were possible. To this end he set out on his two minor missions to Perugia and Siena.

His instructions for the mission to Baglioni – a captain in the pay of Florence who refused to *capitanare* – were to "prick him till he bleeds," and we can imagine how well he succeeded. On his second mission, to Pandolfo Petrucci – the shrewdest robber-baron in Italy, whom Cesare Borgia had called the "mastermind of the conspiracy" – he got nothing from his clever adversary except a lesson in political skepticism, not unlike the one he had once learned under Caterina Sforza's tutelage. He set down the fruits of his experience in a letter which Giuseppe Baretti, the wittiest practitioner of the art of letter-writing in eighteenth-century Italy, called the finest in Italian literature. Having learned his lesson, Machiavelli returned to Florence, convinced that the pair of them had plans afoot to aid and abet Bartolommeo d'Alviano, and take full advantage of any successful aggressive move on the part of that soldier of fortune.

The move soon came: Bartolommeo set up camp in the very heart of Tuscany. If Niccolò took a look at the map, he doubtless noticed that the *condottiere's choice* of head-quarters had put him in a position to attack, at his discretion, either Pisa, Livorno, or Piombino – the three gateways leading from Tuscany to the Tyrrhenian Sea. He may have concluded – as Giacomini, the commander-in-chief of the Florentine army certainly did – that the move had to be countered as rapidly as possible. But we discover, to our stupefaction, that Their Magnificences obliged Machiavelli (who was, as he phrased it, their "interpreter") to dispatch letters first entreating, then expressly and repeatedly ordering, their general not to fight: "Insofar as an attack is concerned, you are to take great care not to tempt fortune at any price ... and you are never to engage your troops in any move that might prove hazardous." The orders of August 16, 1505, were not in the best military tradition either: "Your first consideration must be the safety of the army ... the army must be saved." Machiavelli transmitted these orders, but Giacomini disregarded them and attacked Barto-lommeo d'Alviano at Tor San Vincenzo – the very spot where 200,000 invaders from Gaul had suffered disaster 2,000 years before. The battle, which took place on August 17, 1505, was a clear victory for the Florentines, and Giacomini's bulletin announcing their triumph a veritable paean. (The bulletin was headed "From a most favorable position near Bibbona," thus effacing the memory of certain "fearsome positions" the French had taken beneath the walls of Pisa.)

Unfortunately, this heady victory caused the Signori of the Palazzo Vecchio to lose the little good sense they had. Over-eager to "garner the fruits [of this victory] ... before the troops forget how to win victories," the Signori launched a premature attack on the ramparts of Pisa. The unseasoned Florentine troops suffered a disgraceful defeat. On September 7 the Florentine artillery opened a huge breach, eight hundred feet wide, in the ramparts. But the infantry refused to budge, preferring the prospect of being put to death on the spot by their leaders to certain slaughter at the hands of the stubborn Pisan defenders and 300 Spaniards who had entered the city shortly before – a figure which rumors flying through the Florentine ranks soon raised to 2000. The military commissars were forced to order the troops back to camp, and the army thus set up winter quarters in the middle of summer.

Only a defeat as humiliating as this could have brought Their Magnificences around to taking – finally – the measures necessary to ensure victory: Florence would have to organize a real national army, reviving the old tradition of a standing militia which had fallen into disuse during the century of Medici domination. As Machiavelli phrased it in the last verse of his *First Decennale,* their task was nothing less than to "reopen the temple of Mars" (*"reaprir il tempio a Marte"*), that is to say, to replace the mercenaries by a permanent militia. The job of recruiting these militiamen was entrusted to Machiavelli; but between the appointment of the Seven of Practice on the one hand and the Ten of Power on the other, he was forced to wait more than a year for the establishment of a Nine of the Militia. He was named official secretary to this committee that he himself had created, and gladly accepted the enormous added responsibilities that the post entailed. In his first *Official Letters* and *Private Letters* of the year 1506 we watch him pass from one exhausting task to the next, from the procurement of conscripts to the composition, in two weeks, of the *Decennali,* from facing nagging little worries over money to the writing of a brilliant description of the current situation in Europe.

But the populace, enraged at the disappointment of their high hopes, once again cast about for a scapegoat. This time their choice landed on Giacomini, the leader of the militia, who took all the blame himself instead of passing it on to the real culprits, the cowards in the Palazzo Vecchio. When a great hue and cry was raised in the streets and public squares for Giacomini's resignation, Machiavelli wrote him urging him not to resign, if only "so that this envious rabble will have no chance to get you in its clutches, nor any further reason to howl at your heels." But Giacomini, embittered by his experiences, did not heed his friend's advice and tendered his resignation. The Signoria accepted it, and thus the Florentine Republic lost the only warrior who, six years later, might have been able to defend her, or at least allow her to escape with her honor intact.

Machiavelli now set out to raise his militia. For the next

six years we follow him from village to village, from Mugello to Casentino, as he performs the thankless task of making disciplined soldiers out of peasants whose "insubordination is inveterate," of bringing sworn enemies together under one banner, of ending rivalries "that cut the whole mountain range in two," from Ponte to Sieve. But he brought to the task all his usual perseverance, all his usual flexibility. Sometimes it was the promise of money that brought in recruits, sometimes the promise of glory, and he put both "the humanity of Scipio and the severity of Fabius Maximus" to good use at the right moment. It is only when we have read all the circular letters and messages that Machiavelli wrote to his division captains in the course of this endeavor that we have some appreciation of the enormous patience, the resourcefulness, the ardent devotion he brought to this campaign – with no other recompense than the blessings of the Soderini brothers and the empty compliments of Their Esteemed Lordships of the Palazzo Vecchio.

If Machiavelli the man of action reaped little thanks, Machiavelli the man of letters was better rewarded. The success of his *First Decennale* brought him a veritable paean of praise from Ercole Bentivoglio, the new captain-general of the Republic, who urged him to go on with the work. Vespucci, his publisher, announced to the public that the chapter that had appeared was "a mere earnest of the more extended Work which the author is now contriving within the privacy of his study." A spurious edition was soon being sold under the counter, and brought the perpetrators of the fraud more than one hundred ducats. The indignant Vespucci described this pirated edition as "a miserable cheapjack," "badly bound, with no margins, tiny title pages, with no end-papers front or back, crooked type, printer's errors in many places." We suspect that Niccolò, like his father, Ser Bernardo, prized fine editions. After the Eight of the Police had ferreted out one of the perpetrators of the pirated edition and made him hand over his fifty ducats' share in the profits to Machiavelli, the latter presented the Eight with ten copies of the pamphlet, which he had "arranged to have nicely bound," as a token of his appreciation. The work was again put on sale, "at the stationer's, at two silver *quattrini* the copy." Let us recall here that Machiavelli had written the *First Decennale* in only two weeks, and that the confiscation of a part of the profits of the spurious edition – not counting the income from the legitimate edition – brought him more than half the sum he earned annually as secretary at the Palazzo Vecchio.

His head was not turned by this success, however, for he always considered this type of literary endeavor not a vocation, but merely a pastime, a supplementary source of income. He therefore abandoned the writing of his *Second Decennale* – as later he abandoned his *Golden Ass* – to return to the interests closest to his heart, politics and the duties of his post. This decision should be particularly noted, for Machiavelli here had met his first temptation: poetry. Reaching this crossroads – leading to fat profits and renown as a writer on the one hand, and to a meager salary and obscure drudgery on the other – he chose to return to the long years of unremitting toil in the Palazzo Vecchio that in the end led to *The Prince*, the *Discourses on the First Decade of Livy*, the *Art of War*, and the *History of Florence*.

Let us now leave Machiavelli the man of letters – poet or not – and return to Machiavelli the man of action. In the course of the year 1506 he had set all of the complex machinery for conscription in motion; as the year drew to a close, however, he was again forced to drop everything and hurry off on another mission to the Papal Court. What had happened? Exactly what Machiavelli had predicted would happen, both in the telling verses of his *First Decennale* and in the solid prose of his *Private Letter 72* to Ridolfi discussing the European situation as of mid-June, 1506. In 1504 the Emperor of Germany, Maximilian, had loudly announced a forthcoming invasion of Italy, but in the end he had not come. He was now again hinting that he would "drop in" on Italy, and doubtless the local princes would not stand in his way, preferring to attack him as he left the peninsula, as they had Charles VIII at Forn ovo. The new Pope, Julius II, had not yet had time to strengthen his defenses, and in Machiavelli's words:

[Although] he is in the midst of negotiations with France, which wants his troops on her side, he has leanings toward the Empire, which is as it should be: France's fortune is declining, especially in Italy, because of the reverses she has suffered; that of the Emperor is bright

Antonio da Brescia: Leo X

and new, and the present Pontiff must be planning to deal with him as Alexander VI did with France [i.e. planning to switch allegiances].

Julius II could not attack Venice, for she was too powerful: she had recently driven him out of Forlì again. Since France seemed to show no further interest in Bologna, Julius decided to mount an attack there. Lacking sufficient troops of his own, he asked Florence for hers, though she had few to spare. The enterprise would have been risky even for a prince with an organized army; for a "disarmed prince" such as the Pope, who had only "spiritual" weapons at his command, it bordered on insanity. Both Machiavelli and Their Magnificences wanted nothing to do with the plan. And again the defenseless Signoria put its trust in Machiavelli's proven skills and sent him off to Rome to flatter this bold adventurer and assure him of Florence's firm resolve to "lend a hand in so sacred an undertaking." The truth of the matter was that Florence had firmly resolved only to wait and see what events would bring before handing over so much as a single militiaman.

This mission – usually referred to as Machiavelli's second to "the Court at Rome" – was actually carried out everywhere except Rome. For three months and one day he followed the Pope's advance, through the fertile vineyards of Latium and Umbria, of Tuscany and the Romagna. But Machiavelli proved to have as little interest in local color as he had in Renaissance painting, and he has little to offer us in the way of picturesque detail. (Readers seeking more information on what Machiavelli called "all the delights" of these princes of the Church should consult the travel diaries kept by two of these dignitaries, Paris de Grassis and Adriano Cardinal da Castello; the latter diary is in Latin verse.) Machiavelli does not tell us whether he drank from the fountains of Montefiascone, nor whether he partook of the famous vintages that the townsmen of Orvieto distributed with a lavish hand in honor of the Pope's arrival. He does suggest, however, that Their Magnificences might do well to exploit the Pope's greatest weakness and send him a gift of wine or other regional delicacies such as game from the Maremma, eels from Bolsena, or white truffles.

There were other facts and proposals more important to report. As early as their first interview, Machiavelli brought up a subject that was a sore point with Julius: the flouting of the Church's authority by the Venetians at Forlì, the most recent of many such affronts. "May Your Holiness permit me to remark ... [that] in the cities belonging to the Papacy, his Governors can be seen leaving by one gate and the new masters entering by another." Machiavelli also noted that, as had happened on his first mission, the irascible Pope "grimaced" and "drew his head up proudly" – a gesture with which Machiavelli was already all too familiar. Another day, when the papal retinue was scheduled to leave the next day, immediately after dinner, Machiavelli soberly noted that "this seems hardly possible," and the reader finds it easy to picture "the holy Church Fathers taking their leisure beneath a nearby elm," and can almost hear one of them scanning this verse that Virgil might have written:

> *Vicina placuit patribus recubare sub ulma . . .*

Though again he does not enter into details, we gather that he was profoundly interested in the outcome of a meeting about to take place in Perugia between Julius II – the suzerain who had come to reoccupy his fief – and Baglioni – the vassal who had won that fief from the Borgias. As the two parties halted beneath the ramparts of the city on the eve of their meeting, we find Machiavelli wondering "how this will all turn out." But the melodramatic coup that he was secretly expecting did not take place; instead they entered the city in solemn procession. Machiavelli now expressed his stupefaction somewhat more openly:

> The troops of the Church are quartered near the gates, those of Giampaolo Baglioni a short distance away; the Pope and the Sacred College, however, are much more at the mercy of Baglioni than he at theirs. If, therefore, Giampaolo does no harm to this person who has come to take his territory from him, it can be attributed only to his magnanimity and his benevolence. I wonder how the whole affair will end: we shall find out in the course of the seven or eight days the Pope is to remain in this city.

But the affair did not turn out at all as Machiavelli had anticipated. The lion – or rather the griffin – of Perugia did not devour the tamer; Baglioni was brought to heel, and followed docilely in Julius' footsteps. Ten or twelve years were to go by before Machiavelli spoke openly of the episode, and frankly confessed that he had failed to understand the course of events. He pondered this experience again and again, and finally came to the cynical conclusion, in Chapter XI of *The Prince*, "that these Princes [*i.e.*, of the Church] remain in power regardless of how they behave and how they live."

Piero Soderini

But in his *Official Letter 36,* dated December 19, 1506, this early enemy of the Church expresses (immediately after a prosaic paragraph noting the arrival of six split casks of wine and a load of pears) the following thought-provoking expectation:

> Everyone here is persuaded that, should the undertaking against Bologna succeed, the Pope will not hesitate in the least to launch even more ambitious projects [we know that Machiavelli had thus far shared this conviction], and it is hoped that Italy, now or never, shall be forever delivered from all those who have resolved to devour her.

From this moment on, Machiavelli's anticlericalism (and, similarly, his attitude toward Savonarola) was tinged with a note of respect. As Borgia's cunning had paid off at Sinigaglia, so Julius' temerity was rewarded at Perugia, and Machiavelli doubtless concluded that this Pope promised to be something more than a "disarmed prophet." Reinforcements to ensure the Pope's victory were immediately forthcoming from all sides – including France and even Florence – and the master of Bologna had to put down his arms without ever having used them. When the Bolognese spokesmen who had been sent to beg the Pope's forgiveness dared to complain – "moderately" – to Machiavelli of the behavior of the Florentine troops, he replied with a laugh that it was "the Bolognese troops who had taught them the tune."

Machiavelli had a sharp tongue, and though he employed his talent for cutting sarcasm warily, he knew he was bound to pay rather dearly for it. He was also aware that the increasing authority he had been given was not likely to prove an unmixed blessing. He was therefore not too disturbed when, along with many compliments from Florence, a certain amount of malicious slander also reached his ears. Only one such vicious remark really hurt: Biagio reported that Alamanno Salviati – the man to whom he had dedicated his *First Decennale,* and in whose honor he had written six tercets of justly deserved praise – had declared "that since being a member of the Ten, he had never entrusted any mission to this camp-follower." Was this simply the disdain of an extremely wealthy patron for a penniless, grubbing factotum, or was there another reason for his spite? Whatever the explanation, Machiavelli was to remember the episode and take his revenge. He was somewhat consoled by the news that all was well with the recruiting campaign he had had to abandon for what certain of his detractors in Florence described as "a soft life, doing nothing." This was encouraging news, and on his return to the Palazzo Vecchio he garnered the fruits of his labor, obtaining at last official approval of his project for a militia from the Ten, and later from the Council of the Signoria and the Popular Council, the vote being 841–371 in his favor. The same day – December 22, 1506 – brought the election of a Nine of the Militia, who henceforth took their place alongside the Eight of the Police and the Ten of Power. Machiavelli was named the secretary of the Nine and given the right to be addressed as "Your Magnificence" – the same title that members of the Signoria enjoyed.

Machiavelli spent eighteen of the months from November, 1506, to September, 1508, "at home," dividing his time between sessions of the various ministries he served as secretary in the Palazzo Vecchio and junkets to outlying Florentine territories to sign up recruits. For the moment Machiavelli (whom his friend Biagio described as *"cursitandi et*

48

equitandi tam vagus" – ever galloping about hither and yon) was only too happy to return to everyday life in Florence once again: his family, the baptism of his fourth baby (probably this was Ludovico; we know that a member of the Albizzi family asked to be this baby's godparent), long talks and "little sprees" with his circle of faithful friends. His particular concern, however, was the organization of the militia, for during his absence there had been errors committed that had caused talk. Though encouragement and congratulations poured in from almost all sides, we learn from Francesco Salviati that vicious rumors had begun to spread in Florence. These concerned not only Machiavelli, but the Soderini brothers as well. Piero Soderini, the *gonfalonier,* in particular was being severely criticized for having shown his partiality to his secretary too openly. Ultimately, the very foundations of the regime were called into question. The Florentines remembered how the Republic had flourished under Cosimo and Lorenzo, and the exiled Medici somehow seemed less odious now. Moreover, the current Medici pretender – Cardinal Giovanni de' Medici, the future Pope Leo X – was quite capable of wielding his influence from afar. Under pressure from the Cardinal and the Emperor of Germany, partisans of the Medici in Florence saw to it that Machiavelli's appointment as legate to the German court was annulled, and Francesco Vettori was named in his stead. They also caused the failure of Roberto Acciajuoli's proposed mission to the Safawid court of Persia – a mission on which Machiavelli would have held the post of attaché to the ambassador. Seeking to put down this increasingly powerful opposition without challenging it openly, Soderini avoided bringing the issue to a vote in the Council and took no notice of Machiavelli's strenuous objections. Two weeks later, on the pretext that he needed a confidential message delivered immediately to Vettori, Soderini ordered Machiavelli to Germany. Soderini's jack-of-all-trades again agreed to go; but judging from his *Capitolo sull'ingratitudine,* which was probably composed in the course of this surprise mission, we gather that Machiavelli did so with great bitterness. Though he seldom speaks of himself, he writes in this poem:

> The envy that rends me poisons my life . . .
> How easily long years of service come to nothing,

49

How easily we build on sand, on waves . . .
Ingratitude nowhere triumphs
More joyously than in the rabble's heart . . .

But Fortune rewarded Machiavelli, for as he galloped at breakneck speed through Switzerland during this long journey to a far-off land, he caught his first glimpse of the *Germania* of Tacitus. Machiavelli the traveler not only polished the rough edges of his mind through contact with others; he also compared the peoples of one country with those of another, the men of his time with those of two thousand years before, and from these comparisons deduced man's ideal nature. Ten years later Machiavelli was to set his conclusions down in the *Discourses* and the *Art of War*, but for the moment his task was a more limited one. He was to help Vettori bargain – not with Maximilian, but with the Imperial treasurers – and get them to reduce the viaticum Florence owed Maximilian. (The city states of Italy, nominally still vassals of the Empire, owed their suzerain this sum for the expenses of his forthcoming journey to Rome to be crowned King of the Romans.) The Emperor had at first asked for 500,000 ducats, but now agreed to accept 50,000 ducats. In an attempt to defer payment of this sum and spread the installments out over a longer period, the two legates deliberately wasted endless hours quibbling over the terms. And once again Machiavelli displayed all the patience, tenacity, and artful persuasion that make him the model salesman of all time. And during this exhausting mission he also somehow found time to observe the people around him. From his observations of the behavior of these German courtiers of his own time, he predicted that their distant descendants, and accurately described a "Pan-Germanic dream" that lay far in the future. His analysis of both the latent strength and the hidden defects of the immense Imperial machine has aroused the admiration of more than one historian of the German Empire of 1871. On his return to Florence on June 6, 1508, he immediately began to compile his *Ritratti delle cose dell' Alamagna (Report on Affairs in Germany)*, which he completed in 1512.

Among his *Official Letters* of the year 1509 is a document which explains why Machiavelli seemed to be everywhere at once, and is at the same time an extremely revealing self-portrait. It is a Letter-Patent for a Mission to the Interior, beginning: "*WE,* the Ten of Freedom and Power of the Republic of Florence"; it is signed *NICOLAUS MACLAVELLUS,* and is dated *in Palatio florentino, die 16 augusti MDVIII.* Addressed "To whom it may concern – Conscripts of the General Staff, Chancellors, Officers, and Subjects," the letter serves to introduce "Niccolò, the estimable and enlightened son of Bernardo Machiavelli," and the addressee is to "obey the aforementioned Machiavelli as you would Our Magistracy . . ." We can imagine the sly smile that must have crossed Machiavelli's lips as he received this token of esteem from the hand of "Maclavellus" himself and descended the steps of the Palazzo Vecchio! But the letter was more than a joke, for it not only confirmed his right to command his conscripts (a right he had already been exercising for some years), but also implied, as both he and the Signoria recognized, his right and duty to supervise Florence's last campaign against Pisa.

The time had come to end this ten-year siege of Troy. The necessary measures had already been taken: the various "protectors" of the besieged city had been paid off, at a very high price, and for the moment they were busy elsewhere, plotting a coalition against Venice. The Florentines now made a wise decision: they need not conquer the Pisans by force of arms, battering down the ramparts and slowly fighting their way across the debris, the barricades, the inner trenches. It would be far easier to starve the city into submission. They would follow Machiavelli's brilliant plan of ten years before: Florentine commanders were to be stationed at three strategic points, and each of the three commanders was to be responsible for the blockade of his sector. Officially, Machiavelli was to be in charge of liaison between the three commanders; unofficially, he was to supervise their operations. But one of these commanders was Alamanno Salviati, the arrogant Medici partisan whose attacks on Machiavelli and Piero Soderini we have already described. We are therefore not surprised to learn – from a confidential letter from Biagio to Machiavelli, bearing the salutation "Magnificent Captain General" – that a "nasty storm" has been brewing against Machiavelli in the Palazzo Vecchio; that "all the water in the Arno would not wash the matter clean"; that "this affair has not been well-received in the ministry at all." Biagio then adds:

Those who are most powerful are always the ones who are right in the end, and they must be respected. Experience has long since taught you to be patient, how to conduct yourself in circumstances such as these; tell yourself that this is a matter of little importance to you, since you must necessarily remain far from the scene, and that you can easily smooth matters over by writing a letter or two. *Et superius* [*i.e.*, in the *gonfalonier's* headquarters on the top floor of the Palazzo Vecchio], a person with whom I had a long conversation yesterday asked me to write you this, and beg you to be patient, out of friendship for him. As for your recall, it is out of the question ... The dreadful prospect of leaving your men there without you has overridden every other consideration.

We gather from this that Machiavelli had been taken to task for some reason, and had asked to be recalled. He would not even consider writing "a letter of two" to square matters with Alamanno Salviati however, for the latter's offensive remarks had greatly angered him. The proud patrician first denied that he had ever made these remarks, then apologized for his fit of temper, and in the end made the following admission:

Although the soldiers are quite willing to recognize your authority, you know that you cannot be everywhere at once to command them. On the other hand, I appreciate their affection and esteem for you: since they have your ear each day, they will be all the more obedient and will know what they have to do.

Machiavelli was not satisfied merely to perform his duties as liaison officer for the three Division Staffs, shuttling between the headquarters at San Pietro, Mezzana, and Val di Serchio. He also went in with the troops when they engaged the enemy – an operation that earned him a letter of congratulations from the Signoria on February 28, 1509. Though the bulletins have been lost, we know that he took part in some twenty other operations, including an ambush and the damming of the Arno. We also learn (from his *Official Letter* of March 7, 1509) that his frequent inspection tours had much to do with the fact that troops who had once been simple peasants were now reliable sappers and disciplined soldiers. Their Magnificences – even Piero

Soderini himself – begged him "not to go to positions where he would be risking his life at the hands of these troops" (*i.e.* the Pisans), but such pleas fell on deaf ears. When the Signori insisted that he stay out of danger, he again wrote them a reply that bordered on disrespect:

> I take it from this letter that Your Magnificences wish me to take up residence in Cascina, a step that is to my mind most inopportune, for anyone could serve there in my stead. If I were to settle down there, I could no longer keep an eye on the infantry or on anything else. I am quite aware of the fact that my residence there would be less perilous and less fatiguing, but had I not been willing to suffer peril and fatigue, I would not have left Florence; I therefore beg Your Magnificences to allow me to remain in camp, to share the tribulations and uncertainties of war with the officers; in this way I shall be of some use, whereas in Cascina I would be of no use and would perish of despair; I therefore implore you to appoint some person other than me to that post, in the event that Serragli should refuse to continue to serve in this office that suits him perfectly. (Letter of April 16, 1509.)

Machiavelli had helped build pontoon bridges across the Arno and had served as supply-officer at Pistoia. He now assumed still another function, that of Florentine pleni-potentiary to Piombino, a post in which his services proved even more valuable.

When Pisa submitted at last, the Florentines placed the following inscription on the walls of the conquered city: *Submissio civitatis Pisarum:* In Memory of the Surrender of the City of Pisa. Beneath this legend were engraved the names of the three Florentine commanders; the one name omitted was Machiavelli's. His only reward was the con-gratulations of his friends. "You were by no means the man least responsible for this triumph," Vespucci wrote; "it was you and your battalions who brought about this noble victory – not because you delayed action, but rather because you forced the enemy to fight." His friend Casavecchia called him the "mainspring" of the victory, and after praising him to the skies, invited him to visit his country estate in Barga and promised to save him a "pool full of trout and a vintage wine the like of which he had never drunk before."

Florence was not the only city to light victory bonfires and ring out the glad tidings from every church steeple; there was general rejoicing in France as well, for the victory at Agnadello canceled out the humiliating defeats at Cerignola and the Garigliano. And Machiavelli could see that the first part of Julius' political program had now been taken care of: Venice had gotten the beating she deserved. The League of Cambrai had been dissolved. Every strong-

Sketch, by Machiavelli, for the Art of War

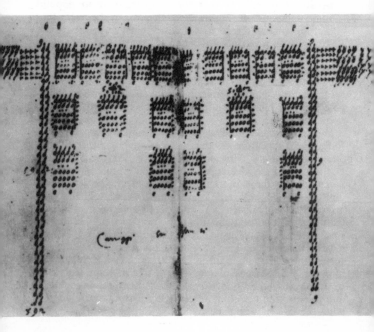

hold in Lombardy and on the Venetian mainland had fallen, and only the Pope had kept his holdings intact. The Papal States had been both reunited and enlarged. But all the rest of the peninsula was soon to become the apple of discord, the coveted prize in the coming struggle between Louis XII of France, who had played every card he had in the recent campaign, and Maximilian of Germany, who had finally decided that it was high time to leave his mountain retreat and go collect the debts, damages, and viatica promised him at Trent. He took this occasion to occupy Verona, Vicenza, and Padua without striking a single blow, though he was prepared to beat a hasty retreat from the latter city if necessary.

Machiavelli had once served as paymaster of his militia; he was now promoted to the post of Treasurer-General of the Republic and sent on his second mission to the Emperor Maximilian. When it came time to hand over the first 20,000 ducats on the debt Florence owed Maximilian, Machiavelli made sure that the Emperor's finance officer fitted the description he had been given of him: "He will be a man short in stature; 30 to 32 years old; somewhat plump; with a red beard and rather kinky red hair." This post should have been a sinecure. But as usual, his assignment was a double one, for again he was entrusted with the delicate mission of sending back secret reports and predictions. His first report was sent from Mantua, which he described as a "dry island" in the middle of a swamp, where he "could dig up nothing really worth reporting, for there are false rumors flying about all over the place." The situation in Verona, however, was extremely tense, for that city was rent with bitter rivalries between the conquerors and the conquered on the one hand, and between French and German factions on the other. From *Private Letter 97* we learn that Machiavelli was in fact reluctant to visit the city, and received a letter from Biagio reproaching him for his delay. But once Machiavelli had arrived on the scene, his perception of the realities of the situation was as acute as ever, and he clearly discerned the first evidences of a patriotic fervor no one had anticipated. From among the various oppressors – France, Germany, Spain, Venice – disputing the right to rule the Venetian mainland, the oppressed had chosen Venice, and had gone to the gibbet with the name of San Marco on their lips. In his spare time Niccolò wrote

– with the same pen, though not the same ink – a series of works so different in style as to seem to constitute a sort of wager with himself: his famous letter describing his meeting with an old woman who made helmets, his *Second Decennale,* and a penetrating strategic analysis of the situation in Verona which he later incorporated in his *Art of War.* Finally, just as he was about to return home, he received a letter from Biagio warning him that his civil rights had been endangered: Bernardo, his father, had been denounced as a bastard! Though his friend advised him to go underground and not return, Machiavelli went back to fight it out, and eventually the ugly slander was laid to rest.

His third mission to the court of France apparently lasted less than three months and twenty days. As we might have expected, he does not even mention the châteaux of Touraine, and does not describe the fine cities he calls *Bles, Siaburg,* and *Torsi* (Blois, Chambord, and Tours). But again we are given a full report of the brilliant diplomatic maneuvers he brought off during this mission, one of the most difficult he ever undertook. He also gives us some hint of the stealthy plotting behind the scenes that eventually led to open battle at Ravenna. And finally, the reports shed additional light on the negotiator himself. At the court of France Machiavelli found a discouraged, exasperated, suspicious king. Louis' discouragement stemmed from the death of the Cardinal d'Amboise, his right-hand advisor, and the defection of his Swiss halberdiers, whose term of enlistment had just expired. (Cardinal Schinner, the Pope's counselor and a more daring rabble-rouser than the Holy Father, was entertaining fond dreams of a *helveticum imperium.* – a Swiss Empire – a project that aroused Machiavelli's fears, for it would give the Church Temporal an ideal militia.) Louis' exasperation stemmed from what had been to him – if not to Machiavelli – a totally unexpected turn of events: the about-face of Julius II, who had been Louis' ally at Agnadello, but was now engaged in "inciting a rebellion against him in Genoa," and sending forces to attack Louis' dependent ally, Alfonso d'Este, the Duke of Ferrara. And the King's mistrust was immediately evident, for from the very first interview he rudely demanded that Machiavelli, the "secretary" of the mission, produce explanations and guarantees backed by deeds, not words. Machiavelli was also made to explain why Florence had been forced to allow

56

one of her *condottieri*, Marcantonio Colonna, to rush off to aid the Genoese rebels. He was likewise asked for evidences of Florence's good faith, among them the aid of its now much-vaunted militia and the assurance that it would be dispatched to any city under French protection attacked by Julius.

We should here point out that the Florentine Republic too had every reason to be outraged at the Pontiff's conduct: he (and Cardinal Giovanni de' Medici, who was later to succeed Julius on the papal throne as Leo X) had recently supported both a conspiracy to overthrow Piero Soderini and an abortive attack on the Florentine Republic by Siena, its ever-jealous neighbor. Though the Signori had good cause to bare their teeth, they were duty bound not to bite: the King was far away and the Pope at their very doorstep. Though Louis and his counselor Robertet spoke openly of reprisals, Their Magnificences of the Signoria carefully refrained from threatening to counter Julius' heavy-handed wielding of the papal staff with *"una buona matazza"* – a sound drubbing. This situation distressed Machiavelli even more than it did his masters. He was eager to engage his recently organized young militiamen in combat, but he had led them into battle only once, during the fierce campaign beneath the ramparts of Pisa. The militia obviously needed battle-hardening, but they would have to be exposed to combat gradually and prudently, in a series of more and more difficult skirmishes, before being sent under heavy fire. So Machiavelli wrote in his *Art of War*. Four years before, he and Giacomini had cursed the lack of courage of the Signori; this time he openly supported – for good reason – a policy plainly motivated by sheer cowardice on the part of Their Magnificences. But how humiliating it must have been for a man as interested in action, as eager for battle as Niccolò was, to have to plead for tactics that were no more than drill-field exercises and a strategy that consisted in waiting the situation out. He was determined to do just that, however, and carried the policy through with his usual ingenuity and tenacity.

His first step was to win the most powerful interests at the French court over to his side; this he did by continuing the annual 10,000 ducat bribe that Florence had paid the deceased Cardinal d'Amboise, with the payment now to be shared between Florimond Robertet and Chaumont. (If

Their Magnificences finally realized that "friendship has its price," the discovery was due in some measure to Machiavelli. Their humble secretary had been harping on this very subject during each of his missions for years, with alternate choruses requesting the "money that is due him," all written in Machiavellli's characteristic key: an observance of the usual politenesses so scrupulous as to be sarcastic.) Having thus gained the good will of the French, Machiavelli had less trouble absolving Their Magnificences of blame for the first of the complaints entered against them, and finally persuaded the French court that the Signori had granted Marcantonio Colonna permission to leave the city only because they had no knowledge of his dastardly plans to join the Genoese rebels. He then began to fight down, one by one, the antipathies and adverse opinions of the Court, and little by little brought those who had initially opposed him over to his side. The French began to see that there was little point in sending Florentine troops to guard Ferrara, Modena, and Mirandola, for Julius could easily breach their ramparts. The militia should instead guard Florentine territory, and the conscripts serve as territorial troops. First Robertet, then the Royal Council, and finally the King himself, were won over one by one, and released Florence from her pledge to send troops. Seizing upon this victory he had just won, Machiavelli immediately made so bold as to ask for a reinforcement of two hundred lancers, for as he explained to the Signori:

> ... if they send them, it will be a valuable aid. If they do not send them, the idea of asking you for reinforcements will be removed from their minds when they see that it is *you* who are asking *them* for troops: we cannot help but gain something either way.

Removing ideas from men's minds and putting other ideas in their place, "implanting" these ideas, or, to put it another way, "brainwashing": therein lies the whole art of governing. Machiavelli's efforts in this direction occasionally met with complete success – as was the case in this instance.

His attempt to achieve the primary goal of his mission proved less successful. He had been instructed to do everything in his power to keep Julius II and Louis XII from

58

taking up arms against each other, and was to forestall an open clash between the two potentates, either within Florence or to the north. Though he did not abandon this task as hopeless, he was well aware of the difficulties involved and voiced his opinions frankly. Those who objected to his estimate of the situation argued as follows:

> [They say] that the common people in France are rebelling at the thought of paying for another war, that the entire aristocracy is no longer willing to march down into that Italy where so many of their number have left their possessions and their bones behind, that the Queen and the Royal Princes are reluctant to allow the King to abandon the Kingdom and gamble with his life down there . . . .

Machiavelli's answer to those who held these views ran thus:

> . . . Ten years ago the same objections were heard, and the King crossed and recrossed the Alps as he pleased, for when a person really wants something, others soon come to want what he wants.

He had already shrewdly sized up Julius II, and he now turned his attention to Louis XII. Noting the deep grudge that Louis bore the Pope, he concluded: "I can make this frank prediction: Either he [*i.e.* Louis] will take dazzling, thunderous revenge, or he will lose all his holdings in Italy." Eventually each of these two alternatives that Machiavelli had outlined came to pass, one after the other.

Louis was about to "cross the mountains with a boldness twice as great as that of previous years" (a phrase that reads like a prediction of Gaston de Foix's campaign in the Italian peninsula in 1512!). Machiavelli had meanwhile returned to Florence, and in the lull preceding Louis' arrival in Italy he found time to draw up his *Ritratti delle cose della Francia* (*Report on Affairs in France*), a rough outline draft of random notes he had jotted down during the few months he spent in France. As German historians marvel at the *Report on Affairs in Germany,* so the French historian marvels at this portrait of France. From the chaos and confusion that lay before his eyes he extracted central truths: as before he had discovered the essence of German power, so this time he laid bare the secret of French strength. The latter was being dissipated in Italy; the former lay latent still.

His conclusions are formulated with the serene detachment of the professional observer whose job it is to see clearly and not be taken in by what he once called "patriotic toasts." But this calm detachment is often tempered with an amused smile. He frequently reports, with obvious relish, incidents in which eminent persons have made him a party to – or the butt of – their pointed jokes. Thus Robertet, remarking one day that the Pope deserved a sound beating, illustrated his point by giving Niccolò "a thorough drubbing," whereupon Louis XII, expressing mock concern for Robertet's safety, hoped that he would not "get a thrashing from the Pope." Another day Louis solemnly vowed before witnesses that he would make his peace with Henry VIII of England; as Machiavelli stood watching this scene in open-mouthed amazement, Louis took him aside, burst into laughter, and asked him "whether his oath had sounded sincere"!

Machiavelli's letters to correspondents in Florence – some of whom were ex-ambassadors, and others just plain citizens – are more spontaneous still. He is more than willing to lay aside the mantle of his office, the gloves, the towering toque (those ceremonial symbols which Metastasio's Titus referred to as his "air of majesty") and swap current news and good stories going the rounds in France and Florence. During this period Machiavelli received, for instance, a letter from his distinguished friend Roberto Acciajuoli, who had stayed on at the court of France alone after Niccolò's departure. Acciajuoli writes: "In my mind's eye I can see Casa [vecchia], Luigi [Guicciardini], Francesco [della Casa, a diplomat who had accompanied Machiavelli on the first mission to France] hurrying to your house the minute you arrive, to take you off to some dark corner or to Santa Maria Novella and get you to cough up all the news." Acciajuoli next expresses the hope that by the grace of God (and that of a certain lady in Tours named Jehanne) Niccolò will get back home "in one piece" – an event that one Signora Riccia of Florence is no doubt also praying for. He then passes on a blasphemous oath he has heard going the rounds, and ends the letter with a few choice comments on the eternal stupidity of the Signori, who are bad masters of good servants. Though many of the letters Machiavelli wrote to friends have been lost, the trust and affection displayed by all his friends – without exception – in their letters to him are eloquent proof of the important role that such friendships played in his life.

Machiavelli and Florence now spent some anxious moments, as they watched Louis rashly launch an attack on Julius II's spiritual authority as the leader of Christendom before he had yet laid the proper groundwork for a spring offensive against Julius' temporal strongholds in Italy. As Machiavelli noted, Louis' first step in his campaign against the Pope had taken place when he officially freed the French clergy and all his subjects of the obligation to obey Rome. His second step was graver still: he had gone so far as to convoke a Gallican council to review Julius' policies and – doubtless – remove him from the papal throne. And, finally, Louis had had the temerity to invite his council to meet in Pisa, under the very nose of the accused! The Signoria was neither willing nor able to admit that an irreparable error had been committed, and spent the year 1511 trying to repair the damage done. Along with his regular duties, Machiavelli was entrusted with this task as well. Convinced – ever since his return from France – that Florence was about to be "caught in the middle" of the impending military conflict, he had already undertaken to solve the most pressing problems of the moment: tightening discipline among his conscripts, setting up a quartermaster corps, buying supplies "at a reasonable price," preventing embezzlement in the paymaster's office, seeing that shirkers were punished as they deserved. He was also anxious to find the right man for the post of commander-in-chief of the infantry, and nominated Jacopo Salviati; his suggestion was not followed, however. At this point he conceived the idea of reinforcing the infantry with a cavalry force, to be organized in such a way as to eliminate the defects of both the French and the Teutonic orders of chivalry. Knowing that there would be opposition on several scores – the main objection being that such a proposal was tantamount to "sowing the seeds of tyranny" – he prepared his answers in advance:

> [A good gendarmerie] will force them to obey. And even if it were the case that a tyrant would thus be born, it is, in all truth, a lesser evil to depend on a compatriot than to serve a foreigner, as those cities who do not pos-

sess their own arms [must do] . . . and remain the most wretched cuirassiers in all of Italy.

He won his point: the Signoria was to have five hundred light-horsemen at its disposal to begin with.

This essential task did not relieve him of his supervisory duties in many other ministerial departments. He personally directed the reconstruction of the outlying districts of Pisa, which had been seriously damaged both by the war and by an unusually severe flood (for which Florence's abortive attempt to dam the Arno was largely responsible). Many other problems were shifted onto his shoulders: repopulating abandoned farmlands, blocking various exports, stopping the coinage of counterfeit money, awarding scholarships, establishing a fair price on bread, moving wheat onto the market from certain granaries where it was being hoarded, for "we cannot approve of the fact that in a year of abundant harvests, there is no bread to be found at any price, and even less can we approve the fact that you allowed wheat to be sold at forty *soldi* a bushel." Machiavelli was serving, in short, as the Republic's jack-of-all-trades, and he must have breathed a sigh of relief on being given a somewhat more challenging assignment: a mission to the court of Luciano Grimaldi, the overlord of Monaco, to negotiate and sign – in the name of the Grand Republic of Florence – a maritime treaty with that ruler.

It was with some foreboding, however, that he prepared to carry out his instructions for the mission that followed, his fourth and last to the court of France. He was gone only one short week – just time enough to leap on his horse and chase down four cardinals who had not had the sense to turn down Louis' untimely invitation to the church council in Pisa and were already on their way. Their presence in the peninsula threatened to set off both civil war within Florence and invasion from without, and bring down on the Florentines' heads both the papal artillery and a bull of excommunication. Three of these unwelcome guests were already in the north of Italy, and the fourth was heaven knows where. Our "good galloper" was faced with the job of stopping each of them en route and heading them off. He was then to ride – non-stop – to Touraine and get Louis to reconsider the whole affair; though the King would probably be unwilling to lose face by canceling the meeting al-

Portrait of Niccolò Machiavelli (?)

together, he might be persuaded to set a later date and a meeting place farther removed from Rome. Though he ordinarily detested playing a waiting game and had announced his views on this subject a hundred times, Machiavelli decided in this instance to mark time. The decision paid off in the end, but he could not escape the conviction that it was a victory won too late. He was not a man given

63

to fits of feminine depression, but on his return from Pisa in November he noted that "the three gilded lilies ornamenting the facade of the Palazzo Vecchio have been blackened by a lightning-bolt that struck the tower," and took this to be a sign of some imponderable change for the worse.

Was Florence about to lose the protection of France and pass into the hands of Spain and the Empire? Were the Medici about to return to the throne in the person of Cardinal Giovanni? (There was good reason to suspect, in any case, that the invisible hand pulling all the strings from behind the scenes was Giovanni's.) Machiavelli merely shrugged off such questions and got back to the task at hand, displaying greater acuity than ever. There was still one of the cardinals who had not yet tumbled to the fact that his presence in Pisa was unwelcome; how Niccolò charmed·him into clearing out is related in the following report:

This morning I paid a call on the Cardinal of Santa Croce, with whom I had a long conversation; so far as I am concerned my sole purpose was to set forth the difficulties presented by the choice of meeting place [Pisa] and by the present situation, difficulties which are bound to become even more serious, especially if they [*i.e.,* the other cardinals] extend their stay there and more people come; I extended Your Magnificences' apologies for the situation, etc. He thereupon replied that the lack of conveniences was of no consequence, and that such privations had to be accepted without complaint, since he was well aware that we did not have the same kind of palaces that Milan has, nor the comforts of life they have in France. But if Your Magnificences' interests or theirs would best be served by moving them elsewhere, such a thing could be done. Contriving my whole argument as I went along, I told him that in my opinion their wisest course was to leave the place, first of all, because they would no longer have to put up with the petty annoyances of their present quarters; second, because moving the council farther away from His Holiness' place of residence would renew the latter's enthusiasm for their cause and forestall his desire to settle matters by a show of force, either on the battlefield or within the Church; third, that by transferring their council to French or German soil, they would find subjects who would doubtless prove more tractable than the Tuscans, for the Emperor and the King can force their subjects to obey very readily, whereas Your Magnificences could not do so at any price.

But unfortunately there were others who did not share Niccolò's ready wit, the art, as he put it "of turning almost anything into a joke." Though the Gallican council did beat a hasty retreat – from Pisa to Milan, from Milan to Asti, from Asti to Lyon – it did so too late. The seeds of discord had already been sown: the council had raised the specter of another schism in the Western Church and in Florence it had brought the Medici the support of the followers of Savonarola.

Julius II chose to open his counterattack on his own ground – the realm of the spiritual – and answered the threat posed by the Gallican council by convoking another council (ecumenical in name only, for most of the church dignitaries invited were Gallophobes), to be held in St. John Lateran. In the realm of the temporal, Julius' plans for a spring campaign were already well under way, and he had won the League of Cambrai, Louis' erstwhile allies, over to his side. A treaty establishing the Holy Alliance – a coalition of Spanish, Swiss, German, and even English cutthroats against their French counterparts – was signed in October, 1511, and with the help of these allies Julius was now ready to carry out the second stage of his campaign of "liberation." While Raimondo di Cardona, the Viceroy of Napels, and a contingent of Swiss halberdiers joined forces to march on Milan, the Pope personally supervised the siege of Bologna. In the course of his famous lightning campaign, Gaston de Foix (the young nephew of Louis XII) drove the Swiss back to their mountain fastnesses, made a forced march on Bologna and lifted the siege, took back Brescia, and won – at the cost of his life – the battle of Ravenna. But La Palisse, his successor, proved an irresolute commander and lost the chance to "swoop down on Rome," dethrone the Pope, and dictate terms. The French now lost the cities they had conquered, one after the other: Milan fell to the Sforza, Bologna to the della Rovere. This left Florence with no defenses against the enemy at her borders and the fifth column within her gates. The Medici now returned to the city they had long considered rightfully theirs, entering Florence either in the baggage-train of the coalition or following closely on the heels of the invaders. Among the Medici who returned was Cardinal Giovanni, whom La Palisse had first imprisoned, then foolishly liberated. A council of the victors met at Modena to share the spoils of war, but the Signori did not send their one available Talleyrand, the consummate negotiator they so badly needed: Machiavelli The Republic of Florence had been sold out to her enemies, and Raimondo di Cardona and a force of twelve thousand men were on their way to take over the city. In a few weeks, the fate of Florence would be sealed.

How did Machiavelli spend these remaining weeks? To answer that question, we could wish for more information than is available from the few rare documents that have come down to us, in the form of a few sketchy eyewitness accounts, several bulletins, and a tendentious recapitulation of events drafted after the fact and signed in Machiavelli's own hand. The very paucity and brevity of these documents attest to the suddenness of the catastrophe; they permit no more than a tentative reconstruction of events. When Bartolommeo d'Alviano had threatened the city in 1506, the Signori had been reluctant to send raw conscripts to face veteran troops, an attitude that Machiavelli had roundly cursed at the time. Did he himself feel a similar apprehension on this occasion? Whatever the answer, we note that the Signori again displayed the same panic terror, again adopted the strange tactic of avoiding contact with their foes instead of standing up to them, even though defensive positions could easily have been set up in the high passes of the Apennines, whose slopes the enemy was already ascending. Their Magnificences even refused, in fact, the generous offer of Giacomini, the hero of Tor San Vincenzo, who by now was old and blind but had nonetheless promised that he and a little band of courageous patriots could turn the enemy back at the "Passo dell'Ostello." We have reason to believe that there was not only lack of leadership; there was probably treason as well. How else can we explain the fact that Machiavelli, who had reported the movement of enemy troops at the foot of the Mugello range to the north, was sent just before the invasion to the south to bolster the morale of the populace of Montepulciano? His militiamen were now well equipped and ready for combat, yet they were not even sent on guerrilla raids in enemy territory. Instead they were garrisoned far to the rear of the crest of the Apennines in the little fortress of Firenzuola, in the insane hope that the enemy could be stopped at that point – no more than a hop, skip, and a jump from Florence. Wave after wave of enemy troops, eager for booty, advanced upon the city. The strength of the remaining infantry and cavalry troops of the militia, already weakened by such tactics, was now further dissipated: instead of being sent into the fray as one unit, they were divided into several small forces. Four thousand troops were sent to garrison Florence's last defense, the fortress of Prato, which soon ran red with the blood of its defenders. The largest force, and the élite troops, were stationed inside the city, which was already overrun with refugees and cattle. It was claimed that such a step had been taken in order to keep the restive Medici partisans in line, for Piero Soderini had been willing to go only so far as to arrest a few of their number, instead of shedding the few drops of blood that would have prevented the wholesale carnage to come.

The behavior of Raimondo di Cardona, Florence's enemy, was hardly less disconcerting. With the fruits of victory almost within his grasp, he suddenly made the Republic an unexpected offer: he would give up the attack (which the Medici were paying him to undertake), in return for one hundred wagonloads of bread, an unconscionable sum of money in tribute, and the promise that Florence would repudiate her alliance with France and put the *gonfalonier* who personified this pro-French policy out of office. The *gonfalonier* and the grand council promptly rejected the offer by unanimous vote, couching their proud refusal in the most lofty language. Only the most discerning reader could hope to decide whether or not Machiavelli's report of this incident betrays a sympathy for this moment of patriotic exaltation whereby Florence attempted to emulate the most sublime republics of antiquity. A similar reticence serves to conceal his real feelings when he is forced to report on "the cowardice of our soldiers" – his beloved militia. Unfortunately, the hapless enemy troops had been forced to go on with the war and again put Prato under siege on the 28th; on the 29th they opened a breach in the walls and almost everywhere encountered only cowards who immediately took to their heels. According to Guicciardini's severely critical account of this episode, the Florentine defenders lost their lives because they offered "no resistance." Machiavelli, on the other hand, begs us to believe that they met their death "after resisting for a short time": among these unfortunate victims were a thousand soldiers of his famous *battaglioni*.

His stinging irony is rather more obvious, however, when he remarks that the terrible news of the sack of Prato has deeply disturbed Florence, "but has had no noticeable effect on the *gonfalonier*, who lulls himself with empty hopes." Yet he is charitable enough not to dwell at length on the events which caused these hopes to come to nothing. When a final ultimatum was delivered by the Spanish on the 30th, the city was panic-stricken: the populace rioted in the streets, the guards stationed at the ramparts and at the Palazzo Vecchio deserted their posts, the prison gates were flung open, and the ringleaders of the revolt attacked the Palazzo Vecchio and took Soderini by surprise in his office. There was no need to attack the *gonfalonier* at bayonet-point, for this leader who three years before had cast himself in the heroic role of a Mirabeau surrendered without a struggle and begged for a safe-conduct pass and an escort to his residence. When he fainted in the street on the doorstep of the Vettori, the latter took him in and later sent him off, supposedly to Siena, but in reality to Ragusa, on the other side of the Adriatic. With Francesco Vettori now calling the tune, the councils of the Signoria brought about the same sort of reversal of alliances that the ex-allies of Louis XII had previously carried off. In his letter to Madonna X, written during this period, Machiavelli did not even bother to mention this reversal of alliances, which had come as a surprise only to the naive; he later added a postscript, however, which was not published until a century later. As sometimes happens, the whole truth of this matter came to light only after many years had passed.

The three surviving documents in Machiavelli's handwriting dating from this period would appear to indicate, all too clearly, that he was guilty of "following the floodtide." These documents have been a great source of embarrassment to those who would make of Machiavelli a bronze idol having nothing in common with the Machiavelli that we have come to know. Machiavelli tried his best to stem the tide and – unlike certain others – did not attempt to ride the crest of the wave until the course of events had proved irreversible, and all was lost. As early as the days immediately following the catastrophic events of the 28th and 29th of August, Machiavelli realized that the Medici dynasty was being swept back into the position of power it had occupied for more than half a century, and concluded that there was no chance of arresting this wave of violence. Unlike the victor himself, he was not at all surprised at the "great rejoicing of the entire populace," and found in this turn of events the confirmation of a passage in Dante, which he was later to quote in his *Discourses*, referring to the "multitude" which shouts in turn: *"Viva la nostra vita! Viva la nostra morte!"* What is the duty of a servant of the State if not to serve it, whatever his preferences in such matters as a foreign alliance, a political label, loyalty to one family or another? He knew full well that at the very moment that Piero Soderini's rule in Florence was falling to pieces, in the ransacked city of Prato Raimondo di Cardona was bringing the Soderini and the Medici around to offering each other "the kiss of reconciliation," and allying the fortunes of the two houses through the marriage of Giuliano the Magnificent and the niece of Piero Soderini. Machiavelli was certain that he knew exactly what was going on and was quietly confident that his loyalty as a servant of the state was beyond question; he fully expected, therefore, to be asked to continue in his post, just as Florence itself had survived and prospered. But unfortunately neither the violently partisan contingent of "madmen" nor the former followers of Savonarola, who "fawned upon their new masters like a bunch of harlots" and began a mad scramble for official appointments, nor even the new masters themselves, appreciated either the value of Machiavelli's advice or the sincerity that lay behind this apparent opportunism on his part. In their eyes his considered opinions were merely a cunningly laid trap and his support of their cause mere hypocrisy – or even worse, the enemy's way of keeping a spy in their camp. On November 9 they removed him from his post as secretary of the Nine and of the Ten, and his all-too-faithful friend Biagio was also relieved of his duties. Machiavelli was further informed "that he must leave Florence for ten years," and as the crowning blow was told not to set foot in the Palazzo Vecchio unless expressly sent for. Ironically enough, when Machiavelli was summoned to the Palazzo Vecchio a few days later for an auditing of his accounts, it was found that the Republic of Florence owed him a goodly number of florins.

"OPERETTAS, IDLE TALES, AND OTHER FRIVOLITIES"

We have followed Machiavelli's career through fourteen years of unremitting toil. He was now forced into retirement at the age of forty-three, and another fourteen years were to go by before his name was "put back into the sack" – that is to say, before he regained his full rights as an enfranchised citizen eligible for public office in the city to which he had dedicated his whole life. This cruel blow came as such a sudden shock to him that for some time he lost his usual keen sense of discernment. All during this first year (1513) of leisure thrust upon him against his will, he vainly sought to secure some position or other. Though the Palazzo Vecchio was forbidden territory, he still had fond dreams of being accepted by the Roman Curia, where he hoped to find first a benevolent protector and later an enterprising patron who would actively further his career. As so it was that Machiavelli mistook shadow for substance – the substance being the minor post offered him by Piero, one of the Soderini brothers, from his distant exile in Ragusa, and the shadow being the hope, shared by both Niccolò and Piero, that the other Soderini brother, Cardinal Francesco, would be elected Supreme Pontiff and remember "his secretary of bygone days." The first of these hopes soon faded, for the

71

papabile eventually elected to the papacy was not Francesco, a man who already knew Machiavelli's true worth, but a Medici, who would not recognize his talents until fourteen long years had passed.

But Machiavelli did not lose heart at this turn of events; he merely clung all the more desperately to his second hope, and thereby suffered another disappointment. Though he did not find in Rome the benevolent protector he had hoped for, he did find an enthusiastic patron in the person of Francesco Vettori, the diplomat who had accompanied him on his thorny mission to the Tyrol. Vettori had played a role in such events as the reversal of alliances voted by the Grand Council of Florence, the fall of the Republic, and the Medicis' return to power, and had garnered his due reward in the shape of an appointment as Florence's official spokesman at the court of Leo X in Rome. On the morning that Vettori was to leave Florence, Machiavelli was there on the spot, and we can well imagine his feelings as he escorted his friend out of the city, past all the addresses from 1 to 175 on the Via Romana, through his own neighborhood, the Oltrarno, to the Gate of San Meo leading to the old Via Flaminia, the road to San Casciano. Machiavelli could accompany him no farther, for he had not yet been given permission to go outside Florence, even for a visit to his farm, and could only watch his friend disappear in the distance, having placed in his hands his new hope for the future – a job in Rome, any job, even "rolling rocks," as he put it. But this friend whom he had so generously aided proved to be both selfish and lazy. Eighteen months went by before Machiavelli realized that Vettori was not going to recommend him; given the situation, he also realized that he could hardly expect to be favorably recommended.

Through an unfortunate coincidence, just as Giovanni de' Medici (who at this juncture was still a cardinal) was about to leave for the papal conclave in Rome, a plot against the new masters of Florence was uncovered and among the suspects arrested were several of Machiavelli's friends. Machiavelli's name was also mentioned, and he now underwent an experience he had thus far escaped: he had administered the strappado and had occasionally had prisoners put to the question, but he himself had never undergone torture. He was subjected to the strappado and other cruelties; six times in a row he endured hideous torture. He came through honorably; forsaking his usual modesty, he wrote Vettori that he had endured the torture "with a stubbornness that amazed even him." His pride did not keep him, however, from taking a somewhat humbler tone in two sonnets he addressed to Giovanni de' Medici from the depths of his miserable prison cell, begging him for mercy. Still, Machiavelli's lot was happier than that of Boscoli, who was beheaded, or that of Valori and Folchi, who were imprisoned in a dungeon for many long years. Machiavelli eventually was found innocent and released. But he remained under suspicion, and was granted only conditional freedom: he was allowed to travel between Florence and Sant'Andrea, his county house in Percussina, and was allowed to visit his barren country estate at San Casciano. Settling down there, he sought consolation in the administration of his estate, in a copious correspondence with Vettori (thirty-nine extremely revealing *Private Letters*), and above all in work. But bad luck still dogged his footsteps and instead of the unique, harmonious, well-balanced work that lay within his heart and well within his powers, instead of a *Spirit of the Laws*, he scattered the seed of his genius to every wind that blew his way.

The justly famous *Private Letter* of December 10, 1513, allows us to share one of these days that to an active man such as Machiavelli must have seemed endless. We see him attempting to while away a few hours felling trees, reading the *Amours* of poets of antiquity, remembering his own loves, netting ortolans to relieve the stark simplicity of his daily diet, spending hours on end at the inn at San Casciano playing backgammon for four-penny stakes with the local lice-infested riffraff. Next we see him returning home, to live what he refers to as his "real life." Having dutifully attired himself in diplomatic dress, he gets back to his reading – consulting more serious works this time – and again takes up the sort of *Dialogue with the Dead* that he opens each evening with the great men of antiquity. He tells us that such moments find him entirely at peace with himself, and so we should like to believe. But in all honesty we cannot do so. We should like to think that Machiavelli earned the reward due him, that he found consolation for his suffering in the inestimable joy of the true creator, that like Leonardo da Vinci he could report that "just as a day well spent brings a blessed sleep, so a life well spent brings

a blessed death." But unlike his beloved Horace, Machiavelli could not proclaim that he had built his own monument; he was to leave behind him only disparate, uneven works, almost all of them unfinished. Upon re-reading some of his best pages, he may have experienced the same feeling of personal satisfaction that he had once allowed himself after the strappado. But just as his poetic efforts had not satisfied him, so his even greater prose works did not satisfy him – in the full sense of that word. When Leonardo writes that mechanics is the paradise of mathematics because one can there gather its practical fruits, he does his own thought a grave disservice; yet the remark is an apt description of Machiavelli's turn of mind. Leonardo always passed on from one invention to the next, without concerning himself overmuch about their possible fruitful results. But political philosophy, history, perhaps even ideas, interested Machiavelli only insofar as they led to action.

The account of his day at Sant' Andrea includes another important moment, the hour when "having left his lands and taken to the highroad, he converses with those passing by, asks them for news of their region, detects a goodly number of things, and observes the variety of tastes and the diversity of caprices that mankind dis-

Benozzo Gozzoli: Harvest scene (detail)

plays." the astute reader will not be misled: in the post-houses along the road to Rome, Machiavelli did indeed inquire about rain or hailstorms in the neighboring villages, but he asked many more questions about what people were saying in the Piazza della Signoria or around the Vatican. He confessed to his friend Vettori that he could not forget politics. As we shall see, the moment duty called he tore himself away from his study, his classical interlocutors, his rewarding work, and galloped off on the most unrewarding missions in behalf of his wretched contemporaries, receiving in return the merest pittance. Serving some person or some cause, being something other than a useless mouth to feed, "a burden on oneself, one's family, and one's friends" – this was what mattered most to him, what constituted his real life during these years. What Machiavelli did not report to Vettori in his letter was the fact that before he conceived the idea of writing *The Prince,* that breviary of the enlightened monarch, he had sought to discover in the works of Livy the guiding principles of a good republic. He now interrupted the writing of his *Discourses on the First Decade of Livy,* went back to his notes, reworked them, took what appeared to be a completely different slant, and in a moment of inspiration drew up,

in Latin, the outline of his justly famous *Prince*, labeling it "On [the various sorts of] governments."

What had happened? Michelet, and later Renaudet, called this "Machiavelli's act of despair"; for our part, we would refer to it more modestly as his "dream of Perrette," the heroine of La Fontaine's famous fable of the Milkmaid and the Pail of Milk. To our mind it was not so much despair as a sudden glimmer of irrational hope that led Machiavelli, one fine summer's day in 1513, to seek out an open spot and there draw up, in Latin, an outline of *The Prince*, a book whose 80 short pages were destined to outweigh for all posterity the 350 pages of the *Discourses*, the 180 pages of the *Art of War*, the 450 pages of the *History of Florence*, and all the rest of his works. Is there anything more natural, more human than this? Machiavelli the man of action had been forced to adopt the indolent life of a country gentleman; he found the chores about his barren estate impossibly dull; his afternoons at the tavern hobnobbing with his four lice-ridden backgammon partners disgusted him; and regardless of what he tells us, his evenings with the *"antiqui uomini delle antique Corti"* – men of antiquity from courts of antiquity – were not enough. Though they helped him to dream of a reborn Republic, modeled on Sparta and Rome, the dream was yet to be realized.

Ten years before he had seen Cesare Borgia, a foreigner, come within a hair's breadth of making Florence the capital of at least a third of Italy – the territory lying between Lombardy, Venice, and the Kingdom of Napels. Though he had no source of information other than the post-riders changing horses at San Casciano, he learned that Leo X's pontificate had been a triumphant success from the beginning: in Rome Leo had had the firm support of his cousin, the future Clement VII, and in Florence Giuliano, and more particularly Lorenzo, the two secular scions of the Medici dynasty, had proved to be wise governors. "This latter" (*i.e.*, Lorenzo), Machiavelli wrote to Vettori, "seems to call to mind the great virtues of his ancestor: a mature mind, affability, intimacy with friends; yet he does not permit any of them to indulge his youthful high spirits." (Members of the family, for instance, were no longer allowed to greet each other with a hearty slap on the back, for it was just such a jovial greeting that had assured an assassin that his intended victim – Giuliano, Lorenzo's uncle

– was not wearing a coat of mail beneath his doublet at the moment, and Giuliano was stabbed to death on the spot.) But twenty-five years had gone by since the Pazzi conspiracy and for the moment at least neither the *"popolani"* – the workers – nor the powerful magnates who had once been rivals of the Medici were thinking of an underground revolt. In the letter mentioned above, Machiavelli himself refers to Lorenzo, the new master, as "the Magnificent" and speaks of "His Magnificence" – both with capital letters. This young hero was perhaps the protagonist of Machiavelli's only *canzone,* and the features of this Captain of the Church were still further idealized by Michelangelo (in the statue facing the "Pensieroso" in the Medici Chapel). If the semi-bastard offspring of a Borgia pope had very nearly accomplished what he had set out to do, might not this legitimate nephew of an Italian Medici pope meet with complete success?

In the first twenty-five chapters of *The Prince* Machiavelli therefore set forth – in axioms as spare as epigrams – the theory of the conquest of power, of the conservation of power, of every conceivable aggrandizement. But suddenly, in the twenty-sixth and last chapter, this cold, lucid, doctrinaire theoretician is metamorphosed into a prophet, a visionary. In this appeal for the redemption of the fatherland, Machiavelli the prose writer reaches lyric heights, and Machiavelli the disbeliever preaches in the manner of a Savonarola or a Bernard the Hermit – except that *his* Holy Land is Italy, the Italy of Dante and Petrarch, with no geographical barriers: "the lovely country that the Apennines divide, that the sea and the Alps enclose."

He was unfortunately preaching in a desert, to deaf ears. Neither Leo X – the most openly nepotist of all the popes – nor his nephews – who gaily abandoned Florence to her fate, the one to become Duke of Nemours and the other Duke of Urbino – took any interest in delivering Italy from the barbarians. Quite the opposite was true: They took pains to establish advantageous alliances with the enemy and thus ensure the perpetuation of their dynasty. And probably they did not even accord Machiavelli the honor of reading his breviary. If we are to believe one chronicler of the time, Machiavelli and his little volume were presented at the court of one of the Dukes on the same day that a shipment of hunting dogs arrived, and the Duke proved himself a man of aristocratic tastes by welcoming the hounds more warmly than the book. "Seeing this," the chronicler reports, "Niccolò went off in a huff, and swore to his friends that though he was not a man to plot against princes, his book would avenge him."

What does the mention of "his book" here refer to – *The Prince* or the *Republics*? And which of the two Medici does the story concern – Giuliano or Lorenzo? We doubt very much that it was the latter, for Machiavelli himself describes him as being "easy to approach at his audiences." More likely it was Giuliano the Magnificent, the Medici to whom Machiavelli had sent the two sonnets he wrote in prison, and after his liberation a third sonnet and a basket of thrushes, this latter being a delicacy sent at the expense of the six or seven hungry mounths to feed in the Machiavelli household. We know that Giuliano was the last man to be interested in governing his people well, let alone delivering them from barbarians. As for the book in question, we also know that Machiavelli had gone back, once and for all, to the *Discourses on the First Decade of Livy,* though each day he continued to revise and enlarge his breviary of princes. Once and for all? – for five or six years, rather. And again he did not devote all of his time to the *Discourses,* for again there were many distractions. He wrote that he spent his free hours *"distractus"* – constantly interrupted by requests for help from all sides. He had vowed that he would have no more to do with the affairs of his time, but the moment that Vettori begged him, in flattering terms, to size up the current conflict between France and Spain, Machiavelli answered immediately. Again he abandoned his beloved Romans, not once but three times, writing letters of three, four, and five pages. These are private letters in name only, for they are full of reflections as profound as the best pages of the *Discourses* and *The Prince.* For a man withdrawn from the world as he was at Sant' Andrea, these writings display astonishingly keen insight. In rapid succession he laid plans for a Franco-Spanish peace treaty, warned against the danger of a "Teutonic tide" (the establishment of a Swiss hegemony), called for a "solid dike" to stem the tide, and envisaged only one possible protector: France. Finally, six months before the battle of Marignan, he was consulted indirectly by Rome, which had not yet decided whether to support France or the enemy bloc (Spain, Switzerland, the

Empire). Machiavelli spoke up for France and against the neutrality of the Holy See, his firmness being matched only by the deafness of those who had consulted him.

Machiavelli and Vettori often exchanged a few pleasantries or a funny story between two paragraphs dealing with politics, and sometimes these amusing episodes were slipped in in the guise of introductions or conclusions. One letter, for instance, tells of a certain nocturnal thrush hunt in the streets of Florence, a tale more reminiscent of Bandello than of Boccaccio. Other letters reveal what difficult financial straits Machiavelli was in, and also show us his good-humored acceptance of that fact. One episode in particular is well worth reading: the account of a feast that Niccolò and his friends had planned, with seven pounds of veal as the *pièce de résistance*. When the bill came, Niccolò could not pay his full share, and left still owing four *soldi* out of the fourteen; a week later he still could not pay, and was being dunned for the amount on the Ponte Vecchio. The poor fellow was also unable to meet his tithes, for the sum levied far exceeded the money he had taken in, and he wrote Vettori a letter asking him to get the tithe reduced. He also wrote as many as five letters in behalf of his friend Donato, requesting repayment of the five hundred ducats Donato had lent Giuliano the Magnificent. By dint of such perseverance Machiavelli forced the Medici both to repay the enormous sums they owed Donato and to restore his friend's civil rights – privileges which Machiavelli himself did not regain.

There are two other *Private Letters* which are even more revealing. In the first of these Vettori, the wealthy ambassador who is leading the "good life" in Rome, does not hesitate to provide his friend Machiavelli, who had lost everything he possessed, with a full account of an elegant party and his amorous dalliances in the Roman capital. The second letter is Niccolò's reply: with exquisite tact, he pretends that he has enjoyed from afar these delights that are not for him; he even rewrites the account in a style that is infinitely superior to Vettori's and says that he is quite happy to have shared no more than "the perfume of the party, the shadow of love." At end of the letter he writes:

When I go to Florence, I spend part of my time at the shop of Donato dal Corno, and the rest with la Riccia;

and I seem to have begun to get on both their nerves; the former calls me a nuisance around the shop and the latter a nuisance around the house. I am still worth something to both of them, however, as a man of good counsel, and this reputation has thus far served me so well that Donato allows me to warm myself at his hearth, and the other party lets me have a few stolen kisses. I imagine that I shall not enjoy such favor much longer, for none of the advice I have given them has ever turned out right; just today la Riccia, pretending to be talking to her servant, said: "Oh, these thinkers, these thinkers! I don't know where their minds are, but they seem to look at everything hind-side to."

Sixth months later – almost to the day – "fortune gave him the chance to give him [Vettori] measure for measure," and the episode in question gives us a chance to revise the portrait of our elusive personage on one count. It would seem that the touchstone of love proved less of a disappointment this time. The woman to whom we became attached was a mysterious figure whose name we do not know, a widow whom a certain Tafani had married after the death of her husband and then immediately abandoned. Machiavelli apparently felt for her something other than the carnal passion we have mentioned previously; in any case his behavior toward her was most chivalrous, and he made every effort to see justice done her – in other words, to get her husband and her dowry back for her. This love affair took him by surprise, for he writes that:

> ... it came over him in ways he least expected ... His fifty years put no strain upon him, nor do the roughest paths turn him aside, nor the darkest nights affright him. He finds everything easy, he accomodates himself to every caprice, even those most foreign, most contrary, to his nature.

This episode provides a fine subject for argument, thought it would doubtless prove as fruitless as the debate that divides the experts in Machiavellian iconography. In any event there is no reason to believe that this courtly love-adventure did not take the same turn as his other amours, nor any ground to suppose that it lasted any longer than his other affairs. We may even wonder whether Niccolò did

not create the character of Nicomaco, the amorous dod-
dering old fool of his *Clizia,* as a sort of retrospective joke
at his own expense, mocking the very same childish foibles
that in the passage we have quoted he describes with naive
amazement. Whatever the answer, let us note that Vettori
slyly "forbears to ask the gallant lover who is going to receive
the bolt-end of red wool cloth for undergarments that he
has had sent to him."

We have now arrived at another of the temptations in
Niccolò's life: that of literature, and above all poetry. Perhaps Machiavelli's *Serenade,* a work which served La Fontaine as the model for his *Daphnis et Alcimadure,* was written in honor of the woman of San Casciano whose name we
do not know. The French poet may have discerned poetic
harmonies in the Italian original that are lost to modern ears
beneath all the layers of mythological tinsel. The same is
true of all of Machiavelli's other poetic words: the *Carnival*
songs in the manner of Lorenzo de' Medici, the pastorals,
the *Canzone,* the *Diverse Epistles on Ingratitude, Ambition,
Fortune.* Though he sometimes shows Marot's talent for
delightful badinage, his poems never have the mordant bite
of Villon or the harmony of Ronsard. Machiavelli might
easily have become one of the prolific raconteurs or
improvisatori in the so-called burlesque or mock-epic vein
such as have always existed in Italy, especially in Florence.
He had all the verve and scathing wit – and all the in-
souciance, the careless versification – that the genre called
for. What surprising qualities these are in a writer whose
prose is so tightly knit! He mentions Burchiello once, the
fifteenth-century barber-poet, and Luigi Pulci, the author of
the burlesque *Morgante Maggiore* whose mock-epic hero,
Margutta, was the prototype of Rabelais' Panurge, three
times. He cites these authors from memory, butchering
them in the process, but they lose nothing thereby for they
have nothing to lose. This is not the case, however, when
he evokes or copies a real poet, an Ariosto or a Dante.
These are the masters with whom he seeks intimate contact,
yet he comes away with no more than a handful of nettles.
He had met Ariosto, the author of the *Orlando Furioso,*
perhaps in the Oricellari gardens where the Ruccellai enter-
tained poor Florentine students and brilliant writers from all
over Italy. (No trace of these gardens remains today, except
for a long street near the railroad station in Florence.) He

had read the forty-two cantos of Ariosto's courtly epic, and on reading Canto 38 – in which the author, like Raphael in the *Stanze,* sketches a short of contemporary Parnassus and names dozens of poets of the day – looked for his own name but failed to find it. He thereupon resolved to take vengeance in his own exuberant fashion. He was careful to mention Ariosto by name in the long ambitious poem, the *Golden Ass (L'asino d'oro),* upon which he now embarked, with the avowed aim of accomplishing a purpose no less lofty than that which Dante had set himself in his *Divine Comedy:* to tell his contemporaries the truth about themselves. One cannot help thinking of Lessing's fable of the donkey who challenged the thoroughbred to a race. After Canto VII, Niccolò's donkey runs out of breath and shows no further desire to "bray, kick his heels, and break wind." Canto VII of the *Golden Ass* is a veritable bestiary, full of emblematic animals even more puzzling than Dante's leopard. Though Niccolò knew which of these bizarre animals represented the author of the *Orlando Furioso,* the reader will search in vain for the key, and wonder how La Fontaine could have found the inspiration for one of his best fables, "The Companions of Ulysses," in such a strange menagerie.

Machiavelli and his great model have at least one trait in common: both these authors loved riddles, a predilection which often makes Machiavelli's *Decennali,* and even Dante's *Divine Comedy,* laborious reading. But Dante's hermeticism always provides some sort of esthetic pleasure and is never motivated by the need to handle some powerful noble with kid gloves or to disguise the sting of an epigram. When Dante wishes to scourge an emperor or flay a pope, he summons them to his tribunal by name. But Machiavelli kept his resentment of the *gonfalonier* of Florence to himself for seven long years before daring to launch the epigram that the name of Soderini still brings inevitably to mind:

> The night Piero Soderini died
> His soul knocked on the Gate of Hell;
> "Not here, fool!" Pluto cried,
> "Up to Limbo with the other kids."

As it happened, two events involving the Soderini had taken place: Piero had died, and at almost the same time his brother, Cardinal Francesco, had been arrested and imprisoned when it was discovered that he had been involved in a plot against a rival candidate for the papal succession following the death of Leo X. Machiavelli no longer had anything to fear from the Soderini, and he vainly attempted to convince Vettori that the two brothers had taken far more advantage of him than he had of them, and wrote that he did not feel that he owed them any extraordinary debt of gratitude." In all truth, however, they had also done nothing to deserve this rude attack on Machiavelli's part.

Discouraged by his failure as a poet, he now went back to writing in prose. For fifteen years almost all of his writing had been done under great pressure, and often he had not even had a desk handy; these very conditions had forced him, however, to master the art of composing even the most difficult messages, full of ciphered texts or veiled revelations, with ease and dispatch. In his *Private Letters* we see Machiavelli completely at his leisure. Though he never bothers to write an objective description of his surroundings or the physical appearance of the people around him, he often sketches a lightning silhouette, paints a lively thumbnail portrait, slips in a revealing anecdote here and there, or captures a whole scene in a few lines. His talents as a raconteur equal his gift as an expository writer, and if the tercets of the *Decennali* or the *Golden Ass* pale beside the terza rima of Dante's *Inferno*, Machiavelli's tale of the "Archdevil Who Sought to Take a Wife" might easily be mistaken for one of Boccaccio's liveliest and best inventions. La Fontaine used this tale as a model for his *Belphégor*, and in this instance the choice proved a happy one; he apparently had this tale in mind when he wrote that he was "full of Machiavelli, and intrigued by Boccaccio." We can only

Ariosto (Arras collection) *Portrait of Erasmus (Dürer)*

regret that Machiavelli did not write more such tales. One day in 1526, beneath the walls of Cremona during the siege of that city, Machiavelli had sought to amuse the *condottiere* Giovanni delle Bande Nere and his guests by recounting one of his stories. The incident was later recorded by Bandello, but unfortunately the episode is reported in Bandello's own words and amounts to nothing more than an amusing risqué story such as we find in the Third Day of Boccaccio's *Decameron*. Machiavelli's *novelle* might well have been cut from the same cloth as those of Boccaccio, Lasca, and other of the best raconteurs of the sixteenth century. But it is hardly likely that he shared the depth of feeling of Boccaccio's *Fiammetta*, nor could he have created such heroines as Griselda, or the humble Simona, ever faithful to her Pasquino, or Lisa, the devoted servant of her king and the inspiration for Musset's Carmosine.

We also see little reason to agree with Tommasini and

84

Dante (Anonymous)   Da Vinci: self-portrait

Voltaire, who rank Machiavelli's theater with that of Shakespeare or Aristophanes. Edgar Quinet proved himself a more astute critic when he noted that the importance of the dramatic element in the whole corpus of Machiavelli's works has been unjustly neglected, and pointed to such essentially dramatic conceptions as his idea of Fortune, his account of the tragedy of Sinigaglia, his portrayal of the personality of the Prince, his love-smitten protagonist of the *Mandragola*, and most important, the latent drama in all his prose masterpieces. The *Discourses*, which again occupied his attention after he had set aside these literary distractions, the *Art of War*, the *History of Florence* (whose apparent incongruities disappear in the light of Quinet's remark) are all seminal sources of drama and have inspired such famous theatrical works as Alfieri's *Pazzi Conspiracy* (*La congiura dei Pazzi*) and Musset's *Lorenzaccio*.

Before returning to the story of Machiavelli's life, let us

85

also mention a slim little volume from his pen that shows him to have been an early precursor – if not, indeed, a herald – both of the modern philologist and of the modern nationalist. The work in question is his *Discourse on Language* (*Discorso intorno alla lengua*), in which he discusses an issue that in his day was far from closed: should an author write in literary Italian or in the Florentine dialect of Tuscany? The philological arguments advanced in this treatise were so compelling that Manzoni, two centuries later, concluded that reason lay on Machiavelli's side and rewrote his great historical novel, *I Promessi Sposi* (*The Betrothed*), from beginning to end, "washing his Lombard dialect clean in the waters of the Arno." If we remember that Machiavelli was to some extent already a partisan of the unification of Italy, his condemnation of Dante's attempt to write in a language common to all the people of Italy comes as somewhat of a surprise at first. Yet upon reflection, we find his conclusions irresistible: we have only to read the three pages of dialogue in which Machiavelli the prose writer addresses Dante the poet in the familiar form and gives him a stiff lecture (though in his heart of hearts he loved and revered Dante), and hear the poet humbly confess his error and pronounce his *mea culpa*. The list of Niccolò's grievances against Dante at the beginning of the dialogue is more intriguing still, for it takes the form of a scathing critique of Dante's opinions of Florence and the Florentines – which were Niccolò's own views to the letter! The heart hath its reasons, which reason knoweth not . . . .

Machiavelli's friendship with Vettori had not stood the test of time, and both his recent love affair (Platonic or not) and the fleeting pleasures shared with friends his own age had proved disappointing. But the sincere admiration and unselfish devotion of a group of young aristocrats was a new source of consolation. It was to these young men that he dedicated the *Discourses on the First Decade of Livy*, his best work: friends such as these should indeed have been princes in an age when those who bore that rank had proved unworthy of the title. He had discussed these *Discourses* with them, at the home of the Ruccellai or in the Oricellari gardens, before setting them down in writing at his country cottage. Because these pages were written for an impassioned public (and an impetuous one), they sounded a note which

one day was to be heard – across a span of two centuries –
by Montesquieu, Jean-Jacques Rousseau, and Michelet,
causing them to see in Machiavelli, the so-called counselor
of tyrants, a fervent admirer of Livy and of genuine republics. It was to warn these young disciples not to let their
justifiable anger get the better of them that he enlarged one

of the chapters of his *Discourses* beyond all proper proportion, hoping to convince them that conspiracies were risky and – more important – absolutely useless. But as in the case of *The Prince*, the work was tragically misinterpreted. Upon the death of Leo X, several of Niccolò's young friends conspired against Giulio de' Medici (the future Clement VII, the second of the Medici popes), who was attempting to forge the last links in the iron chain that would bind Florence to the infamous papal dynasty. Cardinal Giulio escaped being a victim of the plot, but two of the conspirators lost their heads beneath the executioner's axe and others of their number decided to go into exile. Machiavelli spent some tortured moments wondering whether he might not have spoken too eloquently of the two Brutuses of antiquity. On the executioner's block one of the condemned men, upon being urged by his confessor to repent, had answered: "Rid my mind, then, of the thought of Brutus!" Machiavelli should have set his mind at rest, for the meaning of this chapter – which caused the entire work to be published for many years under the title *A Treatise on Conspiracies* – is clear to any judicious reader. Though at times he admired the great courage of tyrannicides, Machiavelli always deplored their lack of intelligence and considered their act useless, or even dangerous, to the cause of freedom. In all of Book III of the *Discourses* the elect are distinguished from the damned with the same lofty sense of justice, the same aura of quiet confidence, as in Dante's *Divine Comedy*. Machiavelli had at last found the point of perfect equilibrium between the hours spent in solitary retreat at Sant' Andrea in Percussina and the hours spent talking with his favorite conversational partners in the gardens of Florence. He had also found the only consolation possible: the proof that he was no longer useless, the hope of rendering a service that would not be a servitude, the pride of what he called "opening a new path."

↑ *The earliest known sketch of Machiavelli, the so-called "Testina"*

Without this pioneer, neither Vico's *Scienza Nuova,* nor Montesquieu's *Spirit of the Laws,* nor Rousseau's *Social Contract* would perhaps have been written. Though the *Discourses* admittedly are not developed with the elegant symmetry promised in the preface, even such a systematic thinker as Taine recognized that this "dust cloud of commentaries" contained an enormous number of penetrating and inspiring ideas, and that "this collection of practical maxims ... seems to have been expressly written to be read on the eve of any great undertaking." "Tacitus writes novels; Gibbon babbles; Machiavelli's book is the only readable one," Napoleon was one day to say.

Again the question arises: to which book was Napoleon referring? The *Art of War?* Not necessarily. There is not one of Machiavelli's major works in which he does not speak of the organization of the military, that complement of political institutions: this subject is discussed in four chapters of *The Prince,* in almost two entire books of the *Discourses on the First Decade of Livy,* and in innumerable passages in the *History of Florence.* In his third work, the treatise entitled *De re militari (On the military),* his only subject is war, yet he does not speak "as one blinded by its colors," to quote one of Napoleon's famous expressions. Though we are not sure whether Machiavelli ever fought in the field, though he had not killed his foe on the battlefield as Dante had, he had nonetheless led troops into battle when they laid siege to a city; he had been a staff officer and an able liaison officer who knew how to get his point across both to his superiors and to his own men; he had organized a militia which cannot be condemned out of hand merely because a thousand of his men took to their heels during the battle of Prato. But he was also a man who was keenly aware of the proprieties and knew his place: recognizing that it would be ridiculous for a mere secretary to proffer lofty advice to generals, he scrupulously advoided doing so. As he tells us in his *Private Letter 206,* he did his best not to play the role of Hannibal's Greek or the shoemaker of Apella.

For this reason he carefully removed himself from the narrative in his *Art of War* and allowed Fabrizio Colonna, one of the bravest captains and most famous heroes in all of Italy, to speak in his stead. Such a technique testifies at once to his self-effacement as a citizen and to his flair as a

man of letters. Knowing that his readers were middle-class burghers and artists who either knew nothing of military affairs or heartily disapproved of them, he realized that the ponderous style of a didactic treatise would make his subject even more unpopular than it already was. He therefore elected instead to write a dialogue which supposedly takes place in 1516, that is to say a period just a bit before the actual date of composition. The speakers are not vague imaginary creatures, but contemporary Florentine citizens whom everybody knew. Though the dialogue for that reason contains nuances which today escape us, Machiavelli's readers caught them immediately. As a matter of fact, one of the speakers represented in the dialogue was a Florentine who had died not long before and been mourned by everyone in Florence. This device gave the work not only a feeling of immediacy, but also the discreet pathos and persuasive force of a sort of last will and testament. In the course of his after-dinner debates with his young disciples in the Ruccellai gardens, Machiavelli had doubtless realized how much more lively a written text can be if it is read aloud, and how much more eloquent and animated the spoken word can be if it takes the form of "friends conversing one with the other." The birthplace of the dialogue as a literary

Raphael: Sketch

genre was fourteenth-century Florence: Boccaccio's company of ladies and gentlemen indulge in delightful conversations before and after each of the tales they narrate in the *Decameron*. The dialogue was again taken up as a literary form by Leon Battista Alberti in 1441 in his *Della Famiglia (On the Family)*, a treatise which won the first literary prize in history. Though Machiavelli did not win any laurels in the competition sponsored by the Quattrocentisti, he reaped an even larger reward in the end. Though his *Prince* and his *Discourses* were not published in his lifetime, the *De re militari* was published as early as 1521; it was soon translated in France and Germany, and was both thoughtfully read and carefully followed by the military leaders of the time. For all we know, the Constable of Bourbon may have been observing the precepts of this book when he fought Clement VII, the very pope who had given it his imprimatur!

During these five years that Machiavelli was fashioning the New Rome of his dreams, Florence had had no consuls, no dictators, no Senate, no Forum, no Field of Mars. Not long after the death of Giuliano, the Duke of Nemours, Lorenzo, the Duke of Urbino, had also died. He had shown no more interest in public affairs than his cousin had, and his successor displayed

91

a similar indifference. Again there were murmurs of discontent among the lower classes, and evidences of an underground movement against the Medici. In 1517 the first af a series of conspiracies came to light. The plot cost Cardinal Petrucci his life and his co-conspirators, Sauli, Riario, and Francesco Soderini, were forced to pay enormous fines. In 1522 there followed a second plot, led by some of Machiavelli's more fanatic disciples – the very ones to whom he had addressed his *Art of War*. But Leo X had smelled trouble from the very first: talk of a republic was therefore suspect, and smacked of the same heresy that had sent Savonarola to the stake. Among the little circle of disciples who had met with Machiavelli in the Oricellari gardens were several former followers of Savonarola, and doubtless Niccolò had had them in mind when he toned down his criticism of the "disarmed prophet" in his *Discourses*.

The Pope now sent Cardinal Giulio de' Medici – the future Clement VII – to Florence, and the Florentines were invited to speak their minds freely. Machiavelli's views were apparently of particular interest, for he was asked to draw up a draft constitution. This invitation was nothing more than an insidious trap, but he was much too clever to be caught in it. His reply, the *Discourse on the Reform of the Florentine Government, Written at the Request of Leo X*, is both "Machiavellian" in the traditional sense of that word and typical of Machiavelli's breadth of insight. His proposed constitution was put together so ingeniously that it would serve as the perfect cornerstone of the monarchy so long as the "beloved Princes" were still alive, yet also serve as the perfect cornerstone of democracy once they had gone to their graves. This is the feature of the constitution that is "Machiavellian." Less typical of Machiavelli is the fact that he was again carried away by an irresistible urge to convince himself of his own arguments, and crowned this masterpiece of clever skulduggery with the second "Marseillaise" of his career. This patriotic paean was as untimely as his earlier one had been, and his constitution was thrown in the wastebasket. This time Machiavelli was not imprisoned in the Bargello, but his rights as a citizen were not likely to be restored in the near future.

He was no better at exploiting the growing reputation his literary successes had earned him. Instead he clutched at any straw in the wind. "I am restless," he says several times in the rare letters he wrote during this period from 1518 to 1520. He sought desperately to maintain his affectionate, almost paternal, ties with his orphaned nephew. When the nephew left for Turkey, Niccolò tried to write him, but unfortunately most of the letters he wrote did not arrive. Though he rarely complained, there now came from his pen such phrases as "What a blow this is to me!" or "I am broken-hearted." Several times he "took the plunge" (as his friend Filippo di Nerli reproachfully phrased it): he would disappear from Florence and later turn up in Genoa, Lucca, or Venice, on missions that were poorly paid but semi-official and thus somewhat appeased his hunger to serve some cause.

He came back from the first of these wretched little missions to Lucca with 16,844 ducats – not for himself, but for the Wool Merchants' Guild. Having observed the institutions of this city, he wrote an informative *Resumé of Public Affairs in Lucca*. His next account of the art of usurping power and winning battles was no more than a device to help while away the time, and took the form of a fictitious biography of one Castruccio Castracani, a fourteenth-century *condottiere*. Though Castracani is presented as an exemplary hero, he proves to be an even more dubious model than Cesare Borgia. How can Machiavelli expect us to admire so odious a piece of behavior as his hero's treatment of Stefani di Poggio, a kindly old man who put down a revolt against Castracani and brought the repentant conspirators to that prince, with the promise that they would be treated with "clemency and generosity"; Castracani then had all of them – including poor old Stefano himself – put to death! Machiavelli reports: "He [Castracani] was told that it was wrong to take the life of an old friend. 'You are mistaken,' he replied, 'he was not an old friend, but rather a new enemy that I have put out of the way.'" We are led to wonder whether this is the sublime indifference of Corneille's young Horace or the comic ingratitude of Monsieur Perrichon. It is neither: it is merely a reworking of Diodorus of Sicily. But it is nonetheless small wonder that Machiavelli's name has been hated down through the ages.

This first attempt at a historical novel served Machiavelli as a training ground for the writing of a book on history. He may have conceived the idea of such a project as early

93

as 1506, according to critics who have discovered that the editor of the *Decennali* announced in that year the future publication of such a history. It is also possible that it was Niccolò's disciples who gave him the idea; or perhaps Filippo Strozzi tried to get such a project started in Rome, as a token of his appreciation of the fact that Machiavelli had published his *Art of War* with a flattering dedication to Strozzi's son; or again, perhaps the idea came from Piero Soderini, the ex-*gonfalonier*, who had made his peace with those persons whom his brother, Cardinal Francesco, had wanted to have assassinated. The source of the idea is of little moment, however. Machiavelli would have willingly accepted almost any official offer to write the history of Florence, as Livy and Tacitus had written the annals of Rome, and such a project seemed far more attractive to him than an administrative post with the Colonna in Rome or the writing of a history of Alexander for Madonna Lucrezia. Though palace life would have afforded him every comfort, he would have been little more than a lackey in disguise; to his credit, Machiavelli preferred the independent life of a writer. We must admit, however, that the florins he earned from the Medici, who finally sponsored the undertaking, were doubtless *"fiorini di suggello"* – suspect florins, fresh from the mint. Though the Medici did not dare to ask him to compose a ringing panegyric in honor of their dynasty, they did dare to hope that Niccolò would keep his end of the tacit bargain they had struck and treat them kindly, thereby discrediting himself in the eyes of his republican friends. But the clever elegance of his style got him out of this second trap as it had the first. In the dedication of his history, addressed to Clement VII, he showers the great ancestors of the Medici house with discerning and well-deserved praise, but we have the sneaking suspicion that he has swung his censer in so wide an arc that it has bashed a few noses.

Machiavelli thus began his *History of Florence* with much the same mixed feelings of apprehension and glee that Tacitus had felt on setting out to write his *Annals*. Following his years of "assiduous reading in ancient history," Machiavelli's political doctrine had taken shape, and he was now ready to confirm his theories by testing them against "the experience of modern history." "Why seek out examples in Rome and Athens," he wrote, "when we have Florence?"

94

Beginning with the very first book, he goes far back into the past, to the Middle Ages in fact, and traces all the evils of his day straight back to two sources: Pepin the Short's ill-fated donation to Pope Gregory III, which gave rise to the Guelph party, and the equally disastrous investitures in Italy for the benefit of the illusory Holy Roman Empire, which created the Ghibelline party. He also gives an account of the fall of the Roman Empire. To him the Empire did not represent the triumph of a true republic, a strong Rome which carefully balanced the interests of plebes and patricians at home so that they would always stand united against their enemies from without and wage just and sacred defensive wars against Latium or invaders from Gaul or Carthage. Instead the Empire represented "a pack of dogs," as Machiavelli put it in a later chapter: factions within the cities of the Empire, and wars unworthy of that name without.

As he describes the first centuries of his *History*, he finds it a rather easy task to "bring the guilty before the bar," and praise those citizens who were great men. But from the fifteenth century on the heroic struggle between classes was supplanted by sordid rivalries between families. These quarrels would perhaps have been eloquent or dramatic, if they had been brought out into the open in the form of stirring speeches or skirmishes in the streets; but unfortunately they were no more than disreputable underhanded schemes for political or financial gain, and the richest, the craftiest, the stubbornest plotters were invariably the winners. Because Florence still clung to its freedoms – or at least demanded that they be outwardly respected – the Medici had gone along with the game down through the generations. All of them, from father to son, from great-uncle to great-nephew, had worn the mask of the simple citizen and the supporter of republican institutions. Machiavelli's difficulties were thus compounded with each succeeding chapter of the *History*, and he tends to solve the problem by wandering off on long digressions. Some of these asides (the adventures, for instance of Francesco Sforza, the *condottiere* of the Milanese Republic who became the tyrant of Milan and the founder of the Sforza dynasty) are informative and dramatic. But others (all of Book IV, for example, which is entirely devoted to an endless succession of cowardly campaigns that dragged on and on, thanks to the "circumspection" of the craven, unprincipled mercenaries) are a deadly bore. But Machiavelli was enough of a historian to realize that his history could not be confined to a series of digressions. In the course of his fourth year of struggling with the problem – one far more thorny than any he had encountered during his diplomatic missions – he one day laid down his pen, then took it up again to write the following paragraph to a trusted and knowledgeable confidant:

> I have been, and still am, absorbed in the writing of my history and it would well be worth ten *soldi* (I would not dare offer more) if you were here with me and I could show you what I am up to: I am, in fact, beginning the discussion of certain details about which I should like to have your advice; I am afraid I shall greatly displease [my readers], either by attaching too great importance to events or too little. Bah! I shall be my own good counselor, and still make every attempt to tell the truth.

And he does manage to tell the truth – or rather, it eventually emerges in spite of his desperate efforts to disguise it! He does not openly accuse Cosimo de' Medici, for instance, of hiring assassins to kill Baldaccio d'Anghiari. But it is quite obvious that behind the little circle of citizens and the *gonfalonier*, "who divided the official powers of government between them," there was Cosimo, who "took umbrage" at the growing reputation of this dangerously popular citizen and all-too-capable military chieftain. In a few brief but telling lines, Machiavelli describes the perfidious ambush of Baldaccio only too vividly, and betrays his own feelings even more clearly when he writes a sort of epitaph for Annalena, Baldaccio's widow:

> [She] turned her mansions into a nunnery, cloistered herself therein with many another noblewoman to keep her company, and there lived and died most piously. Thanks to this nunnery which bears her name, the memory of Annalena – and indeed Annalena herself – still lives today, and shall live forever.

Machiavelli was not always so rash as to allow his own feelings to show through this baldly. But this historian who sought to look on history with the cold logic of a Thucydides, yet write with the ardent passion of a Livy, found it difficult not to let his pen run away with him. Tommasini emphasizes "the great pains the writer took to make his own views, his systematic political philosophy, consistent with the veracity of the narrative"; he "suppresses whole passages that he has set down, tones down the images, tempers the phrasing, sheathes the tip of his sharpest critical foils, erases anything that might offend." This is what makes his portraits of Cosimo the Elder and Lorenzo the Magnificent – the two men responsible for the slow death of the Florentine Republic – models of perfect impartiality. But as Renaudet concludes: "Machiavelli's historical works live on because Machiavelli is still alive in them."

Doubtless he found this literary piece-work dull, and probably he yearned to get away from it for a time. It should hardly surprise us, therefore, to discover that he accepted a job quite out of keeping with his character: a mission to the Franciscans of Carpi to settle a religious question, and the "delicate" task of choosing from their number the monk best qualified to preach the Lenten sermons of the year 1520 in Florence! He naturally failed at both endeavors, and the mission brought little improvement in his financial situation. His health improved even less, for he "found that riding a post-horse at full gallop is not at all comfortable, because of a certain ailment [kidney-stones] that he is suffering from." But on his way to Carpi he chanced to meet Francesco Guicciardini, the governor of Modena, a man who was to become his most trusted confidant, his most cherished friend, his *alter ego* in the last act of a double drama, and the historian who wrote a commentary on Machiavelli's *Discourses* after the latter's death and displayed in his own *History* the same acuity that Machiavelli, his elder, had evidenced in his. We may suppose that the attraction of opposites played a part in the friendship of these two men. *"Con bel cambio tra lor d'umor ei d'ombra"*: there existed between them, Tasso wrote, "the perfect interchange, as between the forest and the river, of lively humor and refreshing shade." It was, in fact, Machiavelli who on this occasion suggested tagging along with a troop of arbalesters who were also traveling from Modena to Carpi, just to enliven this "monkish errand" a bit, and His Magnificence, the Governor of Reggio and Modena, allowed himself to be the butt of their good-natured heckling.

Guicciardini later wrote Machiavelli two letters in one day, and in the second of these paid him a flattering indirect compliment by comparing him to one of Plutarch's heroes, Lysander, a Spartan general who "after many victories and triumphs saw himself reduced to distributing rations to the very soldiers he had once so gloriously commanded." But he ended the letter by announcing that their jokes had gone far enough, and urged Niccolò to come back to Modena, where there was "someone who awaited his return with the greatest impatience" – this indefinite pronoun being a veiled reference to a certain Mariscotta, who Guicciardini was sure could "give the right kind of caresses." Machiavelli promptly agreed to return, and concluded his letter on a similar humorous note, remarking that the monks in the monastery had taught him one thing at least: silence at mealtimes. As for him, he had "eaten his fill," and "stuffed himself as full as three dogs and six wolves." At lunch he would say, "This morning I earned two *giuli*," and at supper, "This evening I earned four," or would remark "What soft beds!" Excesses of ribald humor, and even obscenity, were soon to seem a more necessary safety-valve than ever, for they were living on the edge of a whirlwind. One political catastrophe after the other was about to descend on Florence and her outlying territories.

If the Church, the arbiter of all Christendom, could establish a firm and clear-sighted foreign policy it might serve as a buffer in the approaching struggle between two great power blocs. France, which had withdrawn its troops from Italy following Lautrec's reverses at La Bicocca an Bayard's ill-fated campaign along the Sesía, was about to begin another campaign in the peninsula under the leadership of Francis I, who was anxious to redeem France's lost honor. His opponent would be Charles V, a man at long last worthy of the title of Holy Roman Emperor, representing the combined strength of Spain and Germany. But Clement VII, the second of the Medici popes who supposedly represented the union of Rome and Florence, gave few signs of anything but weakness. Instead of looking toward the future of Florence, of Italy, of the Church, both the Medici popes had sought only to further their own dynasty. On the eve of the battle of Marignan, Leo X had temporized; on the eve of the battle of Pavia, Clement VII followed his example. Such facts must be kept in mind if we are not to be shocked at some of the crude jokes that Machiavelli and his correspondents exchanged in order to conceal their indignation and hurt pride. We must also read such feelings between the lines of Machiavelli's *Mandragola*, a comedy he wrote during this period as a sort of antidote. In the words of the Prologue:

> If this subject strikes you as being overly frivolous, and hardly worthy of a man who would like to appear to be wise and grave, pray excuse him, and believe that he is merely seeking a little distraction in days that are dark: he is not allowed to display his talents on any other stage.

In France this play has not been given the critical attention it deserves, despite the fact that critics have not hesitated to attach the most sinister meanings to *The Misanthrope*, *Don Juan*, *The Miser*, and even *Tartuffe*. In the *Mandragola* Callimaco, the passionate but frustrated lover, represents a transposition of Machiavelli's own embittered patriotism, Fra Timoteo symbolizes the narrow commercial outlook of the corrupt monastic orders, and his Lucrezia recalls the hopeless despair of the Lucrezia of antiquity, for she too is caught in a fatal trap and doomed to dishonor.

But Fortune once again smiled upon Niccolò: his work was staged and was an immediate success in Florence. A friend of his writes:

> A garden beyond the walls of San Frediano was leveled to provide a décor, and an extremely wealthy patron has been offering banquets there, inviting not only the noblest patricians and private citizens of the city, but also his tradespeople and his servants . . . . The borders of Tuscany cannot long contain the impatient rumors of such magnificence; these rumors seek to escape such confines, and will soon cross the mountains.

But the same "very great friend" of Machiavelli's who had complimented him in this fashion ten days later wrote a letter to Monna Marietta's brother, deploring the fact that certain idle gossip concerning the scandalous behavior of the author of this comedy was circulating in Modena: "A highly respected family man, a man of parts, acted as intermediary, but he refuses to name the party involved."

100

But everyone knew who this party was, and Marietta soon found out. The lady in question was Barbera Salutati, the best singer in Florence, the person for whom Machiavelli had written the entr'actes for voice in his play. So far as we know, this was the last – and most ardent – love affair of his life. And if Barbera was really the author of the madrigal that bears her name, we may suppose that she was a more worthy object of his affections than some of her predecessors. In any case, the two stanzas that Machiavelli wrote in her honor in his fifty-fifth year reveal nothing that we do not already know, at least insofar as his deplorable lack of poetic talent is concerned. The epilogue of this amorous adventure can be found in the subtle allegory of *Private Letter 193*. Guicciardini, speaking in the person of a certain Madonna de Finocchieto, asks Machiavelli why he runs after Barbera and her like when he has Marietta, and Niccolò replies, indirectly, in the form of a bit of fatherly counsel to Guido, his young son, advising him to give his crazy little mule his head and let him "purge himself of his folly in the pastures on the heights of Montepulciano, instead of locking him up and putting a chain on him."

While this comedy was being played in Modena, a tragedy was being enacted at Pavia. Invasions by the French would not again drench the soil of Italy with blood for two and a half centuries to come. The news of the French defeat arrived in Rome only a short time before Machiavelli's own arrival. He had long been reluctant to visit Rome, despite his pressing need for money and for the Pope's support for his *History*, a project which that inveterate procrastinator might be willing to get on with once he had seen the already completed first eight books. Vettori, who was as slow at making decisions as Clement was, wrote: "This is not the right moment to request either a reading or a show of generosity." The Holy Father had said, "He may come if he wishes"; what he had really meant was, "He'd better not come." But Machiavelli came anyway, leaving to more practical-minded friends such as Cardinal Salviati or Filippo Strozzi the task of wringing one hundred ducats – "big ones, with a full measure of gold" (*i.e.*, ducats that the papal treasurer had not pared down at the edges) – from the Pope's treasury. The one thought in his own mind was to revive his militia, this time seeking recruits in the rough backlands of the Romagna rather than in the over-civilized Tuscan countryside. He was so certain that this was the right approach to the problem that he sought an interview with Clement, and came away quite sure that he had converted his august interlocutor to his views. On June 6, 1525, the harried Pope sent Machiavelli off to consult Guicciardini, who had been promoted from his position as Governor of Modena to Governor of all the cities of the Romagna. Guicciardini knew his subjects, and knew that they would fight each other once they were given arms. He also knew Clement VII, and was well aware that the new Pope did not have Leo X's ability to "dig up money." Guicciardini informed his friend that the project he had in mind would cost a great deal and Machiavelli, who had now grown tired of the whole affair, returned to Florence.

He again took up the weary task of completing his *History*, but the moment was so unpropitious, and Lorenzo the Magnificent's successor such a sorry figure, that he laid down his pen in disgust. "In the midst of such disturbances a bit of fun is more of a necessity than ever," his friend Guicciardini wrote him. Machiavelli took his advice and sought a little diversion – but in a manner all his own: possessed of an inveterate need to be of service to others, he willingly undertook even the most trivial of errands on behalf of his friends, caring not at all that such small services were bound to be time-consuming and a drain on his declining physical strength. Knowing that Guicciardini wanted to buy another country villa and needed information about the property, Niccolò leaped in the saddle and rode off to inspect two pieces of land in the Mugello mountains, sizing them up with as shrewd an eye as would a professional real-estate broker. And we are not romanticizing when we find a touch of Virgil's haunting *sic vos non vobis* in Machiavelli's *Private Letter* 192; we are simply reading between the lines. Not content with having found his friend new quarters – and magnificent ones – in this Colombaia (dovecot), Machiavelli tried to arrange a marriage between one of Guicciardini's four daughters and one of the young Strozzi scions, but the plans fell through because a large enough dowry could not be raised. The affair provides us with one amusing little sidelight: in his role as marriage-broker, Machiavelli one day stopped the head of the enormously wealthy Strozzi family right in the middle of the street and would not let the bewildered man take his leave until he had walked him as far as the Piazza Annunziata, a square renowned for its sculptures by Brunelleschi, Michelozzo, and Luca della Robbia; once there, Niccolò halted dramatically, and taking God and the famous square itself as his witness, swore to the excellence of the vastly promising and highly honorable match he had in mind. Some time after this episode, another idea occured to him: why not get the Pope to provide Guicciardini's daughter with the money to complete her dowry? Such a scheme was not unheard of, for even the Strozzi and the Vettori had received papal funds for their daughters' dowries. And our Demosthenes now brought all his persuasive eloquence to bear on Guicciardini, urging his reticent friend to follow the example of these Florentine magnates and persuade the Holy Father to loosen the papal purse-strings – a feat that Machiavelli was never able to achieve in his own behalf.

But Fortune seemed to smile on him once again, for the Wool Merchants' Guild offered him a few florins to act as its agent on a ridiculously simple mission. The assignment was an ironic one for several reasons. Machiavelli had just drawn up his *Art of Being an Ambassador*, a magnificent manual of instructions for Girolami, a diplomat off to his first post at the court of Spain. Furthermore the situation at this moment was so grave that Guicciardini wrote him: "We are still groping our way about *in tenebris* [in the shadows], with our hands tied behind our backs, unable to fend off the blows to come." Yet Machiavelli was asked only to go to the court of the Doge of Venice and plead the case of three young Florentine merchants who had fallen into the hands of sodomites on their way home from Ragusa and been held for ransom in one of the ports of the Most Serene Republic of Venice. (Machiavelli had had a similar experience twenty years before: just twenty days after the city of Prato had been sacked and its woman raped in the streets, he had had to spend his time investigating a complaint brought by a prostitute against three conscripts!) But this time the mission proved rewarding in at least one respect: he bought a lottery ticket in Venice and won two to three thousand ducats, the equivalent of twenty or thirty years' salary as a secretary. If the story is true, this mission – his third and last "plunge" – thus brought in much more than he had expected. In any case the story went the rounds in Florence and brought him a letter of congratulations

104

A brief genealogy of the Medici (from top to bottom, right to left): Cosimo the Elder (Benozzo Gozzoli); Cosimo's son, Piero I (Bronzino); Cosimo's grandsons, Giuliano and Lorenzo the Magnificent; Cosimo's great grandsons, Clement VII and Piero II

from Filippo di Nerli that smacked somewhat of sour grapes; at the end of his letter, Filippo bitterly remarks that he hopes that the tax-officer will not seize upon this occasion to "put a leek up his ass and make his ears sweat in a different fashion than Messer Nicia's" (an allusion to a scene in the *Mandragola*).

Messer Nicia was the senile lover in Machiavelli's first comedy – and a prototype of Moliere's Géronte. He was the first of two such characters in Machiavelli's works for the theater, the second being his Nicomaco in *La Clizia*. After the enormous success of the first performance of *La Mandragola*, there were many requests for a second performance; Machiavelli chose instead, however, to write a second comedy. He had already written an extremely faithful translation of Terence's *Andria* and quite rightly decided that if the public liked Machiavelli and the *Mandragola* better than Plautus and the *Menaechme*, it was doubtless because his own work was closer to the spirit of the times. He did not have time to write another original masterpiece from scratch, however, and therefore he lit upon the idea of writing an adaptation of Plautus' *Casina* (which in turn was an adaptation of a Greek play). He retitled the play *La Clizia*, and shifted the background of the action from Athens to Florence. The fact that the Greek *Clizia* had been twice transplanted – first to Rome, then to Florence – did no harm to the play. On the contrary: as in the case of *Volpone*, the work was thereby improved. It does not exude the same air of bitterness as the *Mandragola* and on hearing it performed one is not reminded at all of Henri Becque's *Ravens* or Molière's *Misanthrope*; it resembles, rather, Molière's *Knavery of Scapin* or his *Amphitryon*, though Machiavelli's ribaldry is somewhat more frank. The play was a triumph both for the author and for Barbera Salviati, from whom Machiavelli had written the libretto, and perhaps the score, of the comedy's five entr'actes with dances and songs. And if we are to believe Filippo di Nerli, this singer was also responsible for the fact that election officials in the Signoria finally put Machiavelli's name back in the "sack." "Long live la Barbera. She takes much better care of me than the Emperor does!" Niccolò wrote. And he thus takes his leave of literature with a burst of laughter, just as less than two years later he was to breathe his last with a joke on his lips. He now put literature, the writing of these divertissements which he called "trifles and operettas," behind him to take up active life once again, to live once more the history of his own time rather than that of ages dead and gone.

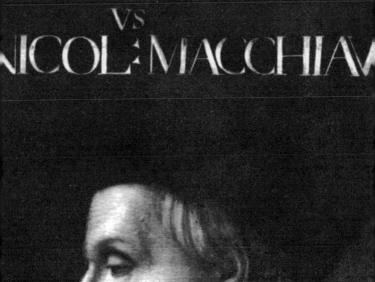

VS
NICOL: MACCHIAV

"I FEEL MYSELF GROWING WEARY..."

Europe, Italy, Rome, and Florence were all experiencing one of the most dramatic moments in their history. The principal powers in Italy had grown weary of the oppression they had been made to endure at the hands of Charles V, and sought to rid themselves of the imperial yoke. On June 12, 1526, a treaty of alliance, establishing the Holy League of Cambrai, was signed by Francis I, Henry VII, Clement VII, Venice, and Milan (following a premature uprising the Milanese had been driven back within the walls of Milan and were being besieged by the Spaniards). The League ended in a most wretched – and most spectacular – failure: Rome was captured and sacked by the Imperial troops, and in Florence the Medici dynasty was overthrown and the Republic re-established.

Late in 1525, Machiavelli had just missed being appointed secretary to Cardinal Salviati at the court of Spain; historians are thus deprived of a portrait of Charles V from his pen, a portrait that undoubtedly would have proved a worthy companion-piece to his description of Maximilian of Austria. The diplomat chosen in his stead was Baldassare Castiglione, a more experienced courtier. The month of April, 1526, finally brought Machiavelli an official post in the service of the Medici dynasty, which was soon to fall. Though this post entitled him to fewer official privileges than those enjoyed by an embassy attaché, the actual powers of the office were greater.

Seeing how badly their captains conducted maneuvers in

the field, and how undisciplined a lot their troops were, the Florentines had realized that it would be wise to strengthen the city's fortifications. On April 4th, a plan was approved by Clement VII; in May, a Council of Inspectors of the Ramparts was created and Machiavelli, who had regained his right to hold public office, was elected Secretary – that is to say prime mover – of the project.

He had great difficulty getting such a vast undertaking under way, however, for military necessities and the Pope's financial interests did not coincide. Motivated partly by sheer inertia and partly by gross cupidity, the Pope contravened the explicit advice of technicians and the urgent warnings of Machiavelli and Guicciardini and insisted on enclosing all of the San Miniato hillside within the new ramparts. The increased value of the papal property thus enclosed was to bring the Pope a profit of 80,000 ducats. The architects and the *condottieri* finally agreed on the details of the project, Machiavelli drew up a magnificent master-plan, and the work started. His fellow-citizens, particularly those who had homes along the Arno, watched him supervise what seemed to them a sacrilegious destruction. As Tommasini writes:

> Seeing the fine, lofty watchtowers of the ramparts, which had stood for centuries, torn down was a disagreeable sight .... seeing edifices considered sacred disappearing beneath the pick and sledge-hammer seemed to others an even graver wrong than the destruction of their homes .... the cloister of the nuns of San Niccolò was beautiful, yet it was condemned ... and likewise a church near the Postiera alla Giustizia .... They had to put up a wall in front of houses that overlooked the Arno, along the riverbanks near the Ponte della Carraia, in order to avoid a treacherous attack from this quarter. Those inhabitants whose view was thus cut off were aggrieved and suspicious. And finally, the ascetics, the disciples of Savonarola, saw in these material defenses a proof of little trust in divine aid.[1]

As a happened before in 1512, the wrath of the populace was directed not so much against those who would serve to gain by the invasion as against those who did their best to

[1] *La vita e gli scritti di Niccolò Machiavelli* (Roma, Prof. P. Maglione, Succ di E. Loescher, 1911), Vol. I, parte 1, pp. 846-847).

defend the city. Our Secretary to the Inspectors of the Ramparts had purchased a superb register in which to record his minutes and bulletins, duly dedicated to "JHS, Mary, and Saint John the Baptist, advocate and protector of our city," but he filled no more than a few pages of it. On June 8, 1526, he closed the huge register and assumed his post with the army of the Holy League, doubtless serving as Guicciardini's aide-de-camp, for the latter had been promoted from the rank of super-governor to that of lieutenant-general. On the 13th or the 15th, a letter from Machiavelli to Bartolommeo Cavalcanti is headed: "From the army." A short time later Vettori sent him a letter bearing the address "beneath the walls of Milan," in answer to his express request for a detailed account of a certain "day when spurs were won" by the Sienese; they too had been besieged, by papal troops, but had cut them to ribbons and pursued them for more than twenty miles. In this letter we also learn that "the French have delayed so long in sending up reinforcements that people in Florence are beginning to doubt the King's good will." Machiavelli explains the reason for this in *Private Letter 217*, a sober and biting critique of the situation, which bears no date and no signature but was undoubtedly addressed to his fervent disciple Bartolommeo Cavalcanti: "The Pope, hoping to end the war in two weeks, started the campaign before the King of France had sent his troops to Italy." In no other letter does he express so strongly his refusal to give up hope even though the situation is hopeless. Among the many cheering letters he wrote to Their Magnificences and to his disciple, this is unfortunately the only one that has come down to us. Cavalcanti writes that these letters are "like oracles, and the presence of his master and conversation with him – when he is there – are a source of comfort and of wisdom to him."

This testimonial should be set alongside the posthumous tribute that Luigi Alamanni, who had been sent into exile, wrote on learning of Machiavelli's death:

Since the esteemed Secretary's soul is now on high,
And his mortal remains are buried here below,
O death! I fear thy cruel arms no more;
He it was who made my life worth while
I feared thy rude assaults only because of him
Since thou hast taken him from me, where is thy sting?

111

On August 7th, Roberto Acciajuoli wrote Guicciardini from Poissy, congratulating him on having engaged Machiavelli "to discipline the infantry, and may God grant that his intentions be fulfilled, though I fear that they will share the same fate' as Plato's Republic." The authority of Guicciardini, Acciajuoli, and Alamanni obviously carries much more weight with historians than do the idle tales of Bandello, the novella-writer, which for too many years were taken at face value. As Bandello tells it, Machiavelli was drilling troops on the field beneath the walls of Milan – or of Cremona – on this very same date. For two hours he had been vainly struggling to get the men of one *bandeira* back in ranks when Giovanni delle Bande Nere, having reached the end of his patience, bawled out a single command, and his trumpeter a single bugle note, which accomplished on the field what had been a mere idea in Machiavelli's mind. Whatever the truth of this anecdote may be, we know that he was sent to the ramparts of Cremona on September 10th, and on the 13th drew up orders for the assault of this stronghold that had been put under siege at an inopportune moment. The troops were either to conquer the city within five days, or abandon the attack and hasten elsewhere.

Cremona capitulated ten days later, on the 23rd, but it was too late. On September 19th, "at the very moment that everything was crashing down upon us," Clément VII was taken prisoner – "like a street-urchin" – by Ugo de Moncada, a Spanish captain, and the city had a foretaste of the severe pillaging that was to befall her ten months later. The Pope was forced to produce the famous "penful of ink": a declaration of a four-month truce and the surrender of the "thousand footsoldiers [that he had said were] all he needed to ensure his safety" – and the safety of Rome. It was the Pope who was primarily responsible for the policy of calculated delay, as earlier he had been responsible for the premature attack on the enemy and the lack of coordination among those seeking to defend the peninsula. In an attempt to lift the siege of Milan, troops were marched 58 miles to besiege Cremona, 85 miles to Genoa, and 212 miles to Siena! Machiavelli's bitterness on this occasion is understandable. The man who had helped him publish his treatise on military strategy had not bothered to read it, and had violated one of its cardinal rules: one must never risk all one's fortunes without risking all one's forces.

But the crowning blow was to come from a different quarter. A few months before, Machiavelli had had another of the brilliant ideas which were often the target of much friendly bantering on Guicciardini's part: he had vainly tried to enlist the Pope's secret aid in "raising the banner of adventure" and supporting the only captain in all of Italy "whom all the soldiers would follow wholeheartedly, whom the Spaniards feared and esteemed even more . . . a most daring and audacious leader, with very broad views, and capable of undertaking the most noble enterprises": Giovanni delle Bande Nere, the son of Caterina Sforza. But Frederico Gonzaga, the degenerate son of the Lion of Fornovo, led Giovanni into a treacherous ambush in the swamps of Serraglio Borgoforte. Giovanni was fatally wounded on November 26th, and died on the 30th. That very day the Eight of Practice sent Machiavelli on an urgent errand, just as in the old days. He was to gallop off post-haste to Modena and for the first time conduct diplomatic negotiations with his friend Guicciardini. "Knowing his probity to be equal to the task," Their Magnificences did not bother to give him formal instructions for the mission. The destiny of Tuscany and of Florence was left in their hands, and they were given full power to bargain or to hold out, as they saw fit. We can well imagine how eagerly Machiavelli began his mission after receiving such an expression of confidence. Leaping into the saddle, he rode all night – despite the troublesome ailment we have already mentioned – so as to arrive "just as dawn was breaking." A cursory reading of the two *Official Letters* written during this mission reveals no trace of the note of high purpose that marks his other letters. But the reason becomes clear when we read the brief post-script to the first letter, in which he announces the death of Giovanni delle Bande Nere, his hero, the only captain in Italy who knew how to conduct the sort of lightning campaign Gaston de Foix had once waged. The postscript reads: "Your Magnificences have doubtless learned of the death of Signor Giovanni, whose passing is mourned by everyone here." What this dry matter-of-fact tone reveals is not a lack of feeling on Machiavelli's part; it is, rather, a measure of how deeply Giovanni's death had touched him.

He therefore said no more, and merely forwarded Their Magnificences an intelligence report informing them that if Freundsberg's footsoldiers, coming down from Germany,

School of Clouet: Charles de Bourbon

and Moncada's Spanish troops, coming up from Rome to meet their compatriots who had finally subjugated Milan, had not already joined forces, they soon would. But instead of cutting off the enemy, the leader of the papal troops "tagged along after them in their baggage-train." The man responsible for such a piece of "strategy" was Francesco Maria della Rovere, the Duke of Urbino; because he suffered from chronic gout, della Rovere "led" this strange sort of campaign from a litter, and liked to think of himself as a Fabius the Temporizer. In Machiavelli's opinion there was no use trying to win the Germans over and make a deal with them: "Germany and Spain are now one single body." A prophetic vision! Niccolò announced that he was returning to Florence "one day at a time, so as not to tire himself needlessly." The two armies had joined forces. In the face of this danger, the Signoria called on Machiavelli once again and sent him post-haste to Guicciardini – who had resigned his governorship because he no longer wanted to serve "an ass" (the Pope!), and then had gone back to his post. "I now am neither a lieutenant nor a drayman," he said, "for I no longer conduct a war and drive neither oxen nor asses. A curse on him who has more fear of danger than of evil!"

These two friends, these two historians of Florence who were the real creators of modern historiography, spent the eighty days of this last mission side by side, endeavoring with all their heart, all their intelligence, to shield their country from the "vicious kicks" of those whom Niccolò called in Latin "savage beasts who do not resemble men at all, save for their faces." With the enemy about to descend upon them, morale of the lower classes in the rural areas, in the cities of Tuscany, and in the surrounding marches of the Romagna, was high: they knew the enemy for the monsters they were. As he had done twenty-five years before, Machiavelli wrote Their Magnificences that the inhabitants "will choose to die rather than endure such infamies and see themselves, despite capitulations signed in good and due faith, first forced to pay a ransom, then pillaged." He also noted another fact: Though the men in the ranks were formidable warriors, their leaders were the victims of the same procrastination that had paralyzed the chiefs of the League and the Pope. During the two months and a half of this pseudo-campaign, he was to notice that both adversaries were stopped dead in their tracks by the same depressing lack of courage, the same fear of battle, that he had stigmatized in his *History of Florence*, calling such campaigns "cowardly wars." He sent the Signoria detailed – and amazingly accurate – predictions of the future movements of the enemy's huge motley army. He estimated the intentions and the needs of its general staff, outguessed

Giovanni delle Bande Nere

its feints, weighed possible routes of attack, possible supply
lines. All this was done with one view in mind: reassuring
the Signori without relaxing their vigilance, inspiring confidence – the mother of courage –, keeping up the necessary
appearances as each peril arose, exposing the snares, pointing
out the right moments for action.

But his advice was not heeded, the right moments were
allowed to go by, and the trap was sprung. Though Clement
VII had already had one narrow escape, he let himself be
caught a second time. The Constable of Bourbon – a former
vassal of Francis I who had turned traitor and was now the
leader of Charles V's imperial troops – kept playing cat and
mouse with the Pope and his troops, offering time and again

to sign a truce. Though Machiavelli and Guicciardini were
on to his scheme, it nevertheless had a demoralizing effect:
he demanded first 40,000 ducats, then 100,000, and his
price kept going up while the already shaky morale of the
defending troops kept going down. They passed up one
good chance after another, failing to seize upon a number
of opportunities, each better than the last, to defend themselves and mount a counterattack. In mid-March a mutiny
broke out among the German troops. Hearing them shout
for "Money, Money, Bourbon coward," Machiavelli was reminded of the similar violent revolt of the Swiss troops
beneath the ramparts of Pisa. The Constable of Bourbon
escaped, but Freundsberg, the leader and organizer of the
German footsoldiers who had tried to act as a mediator

during the mutiny, died of a stroke of apoplexy. For twelve days, from the 18th to the 30th, the March snowfall grew heavier and heavier, pinning the invading troops at the foot of the Apennines, which they had planned to cross on the 15th of March. "And so it happens," Machiavelli reported, "that the barrier that we could not and did not erect in the path of the enemy was erected by God! Would that we could take advantage of this happpenstance!" But they took no more advantage of divine aid than they had of the mutiny of the German footsoldiers. Guicciardini and his aide-de-camp pleaded with the Duke of Urbino to get moving, but he refused to budge and even their rudest remarks did not put a stop to his empty blustering. Reports of two successful skirmishes and news that the French troops of the Marquis de Saluces were "performing miracles at Berzighella" went unheeded: not one of these advantages was exploited. The Florentines were waiting for the enemy to starve, grow discouraged, and go off somewhere, anywhere, so long as it was not Tuscany. The final indignity came when the Duke of Urbino abandoned his command post and went home to cure his gout.

For a time, however, it was thought that all was not yet lost. Instead of crossing the Apennines by the direct route from Bologna to Florence, the enemy took the long way around, slowly making their way toward Imola and Faenza, the gateway to other, easier invasion routes. Machiavelli now remembered that this had been Cesare Borgia's tactic in 1502, when he had prolonged his stay in Cesena and deliberately postponed a decisive battle in order to wear down the nerves of his anxious adversaries and thus further his own designs. But this time it was not Capua's turn to wonder what fate had in store; it was Rome and Florence who waited to see "which way this tide would run" – toward the Arno or toward the Tiber. The Spaniards and the Germans had just taken a formal oath, in the presence of the Constable of Bourbon, to fight to the end and hang anyone who sued for peace – including de Lannoy, the Viceroy of Naples, who was on his way to Rome to negotiate a peace treaty with the Pope. While the Romans were agreeing among themselves that "the sacking of Florence will be our salvation," the Florentines were saying, "Let's hope it's Rome's turn."

Machiavelli, for his part, was repelled by such cowardice,

and wrote a scathing denunciation of this unilateral armistice, which "our simpleton" (Clement VII) fondly hoped would divert the torrent of imperial troops and set them on the march against his own allies. "A truce signed in Rome and violated in Lombardy!... In case the enemy advances, think only of war and let not the thought of peace disturb a single hair of your head; if the enemy doesn't stir, drop all thought of war and think only of peace," Machiavelli commented bitterly. When Vettori wrote him that in Tuscany, "they won't defend so much as an oven," Machiavelli wrote back that it was not the enemy who would get a roasting.

Turning his attention to the many passes through which the invasion might come, he pointed out in each case a natural barrier along which the lines of defense should be laid out. Upon receiving news that the Pope had surrendered unconditionally to the Viceroy of Naples and handed over all his troops, Machiavelli held his temper and merely replied:

> ...that Messer Francesco [Guicciardini] has resolved, come what may, to defend the Romagna so long as he believes it can be defended with sixteen *soldi* as against one *lira*; and if it cannot be so defended, he has resolved to abandon it and march down to Florence and her outlying districts with all the troops he has at his command and all the money he has left, to defend it and save it, whatever the cost.

It appeared that the Constable of Bourbon had decided to march on Florence, either by way of the Val di Marecchia, or via another route which also led to Borgo San Sepolcro (and the Val di Chiana). Machiavelli's icy comment on this turn of events reads as follows:

> Invasion was an evil long foreseen. Surely Your Magnificences can have no reason to fear it.... Our troops are so well-placed, and so many roads lie open before them that they will be at their posts before they [*i.e.*, the enemy troops] arrive.... It is said that men make a virtue of necessity, but where there was virtue before there was necessity, virtue increases and becomes invincible: hitherto Your Magnificences and the city of Florence have defended and saved Lombardy and the Romagna; now you must save yourselves.

(A message no different from any other official lie from GHQ, from the time of Julius Caesar's Gallic campaigns to Foch in the swamps of Saint-Gond!)

On April 26, 1527, the troops of the Duke of Urbino were approaching Florence and a band of rash young Medici bastards galloped off to join the Duke and his staff. This sally very nearly caused the fall of the Medici dynasty then and there, instead of a few weeks later, for the people of Florence thought that their princes were deserting them and rioted in the Piazza della Signoria. This uprising is known as the Friday Riot. The misunderstanding was finally

Print showing Rome prior to the construction of Saint Peter's and Bernini's colonnade

cleared up and the only thing that "fell" was a few paving-stones dropped from the top of the tower, and the only casualty Michelangelo's statue of David, for one of its arms was broken off and brandished by the rioters. But if we may believe Machiavelli's most recent biographer, the Republican sympathizers may have thought that Machiavelli – and Guicciardini – were among those seeking to turn the city over to a tyrant once again. The Republicans were later to remember this incident.

A final melodramatic reversal of fortune took place on May 2. Once they had crossed the Apennines and reached

the Val di Chiana, the enemy army had no further difficulty deciding whether to attack Florence, a city which had bared its teeth, or Rome, an open city. The morale of the Catholic Emperor's hard-bitten old veterans was as high as that of the Lutheran troops of the now-dead Freundsberg had been; eager for battle, they proceeded to cross the plains of Umbria in a series of forced marches. Machiavelli and Guicciardini gave up the attempt to follow them after they reached Orvieto, and the two of them went back to Florence.

Rome was won without striking a blow, and there now began the *infernalità crudele* – the cruel horrors of Hell – that Benvenuto Cellini describes in his *Memoirs*. The passage linking the Vatican and the Castel Sant' Angelo was the only thing that saved the pope from falling into the hands of his assailants. But (as Cellini proudly informs us) the Constable of Bourbon did not escape the careful musket-shot that Benvenuto aimed at him from the top of the battlements.

On the 11th the news of the sack of Rome reached Florence; on the 16th the Grand Council of the People was re-established. On the following day, the 17th, the Medici stole furtively out of the city instead of waiting to be driven out for a third time (*terza cacciata!*). The two petty puppet-tyrants were quietly replaced by an undistinguished phantom republic, in which there was no place for Machiavelli. He and Guicciardini refused to desert their master, however, and did everything in their power to help Clement escape from the Castel Sant' Angelo – this despite the fact that he and they had been "tarred with the same brush." The plan to rescue the Pope is the subject of Machiavelli's last *Private Letter*. In this letter, dated May 22, 1527, he informs Guicciardini that there is a battle still to be won, and that Andrea Doria, the admiral of the papal fleet, has agreed to help. Soldiers are to be put ashore, and Machiavelli recommends that their second day's march end either at Monte Mario (the Roman Champ de Mars) or in the Pope's vineyards. This was the last battle Machiavelli ever dreamed of waging, but like so many others, it was never fought and Clement VII was not rescued.

It was also the last time he ever made the journey back to Florence. We do not know whether he set out by sea, aboard the brigantine or one of the three galleys that the great Genoese mariner put at the disposal of the Marquise of Mantua, or whether he traveled by horseback as he usually did. His traveling companions are said to have heard Machiavelli "utter many a sigh on hearing the news that the city was once again free," and heard him curse "the Holy Father's simple-mindedness." This reference is a last rare glimpse of Machiavelli, for almost all of the remaining days of his life are shrouded in obscurity.

On June 10, he witnessed the election of a *gonfalonier*, Capponi, the re-establishment of the republican institutions of the Eight and the Ten (of War), and the appointment of a Secretary. Twelve days later, on June 22, 1527, Machiavelli died in his house in the Oltrarno. The cause of his death is still a matter of conjecture: was it a broken heart, acute peritonitis, a chronic gastric ulcer? Even today there is no one answer to this enigma. The same is true of the centuries-old quarrel raised by the brief announcement of his death by his son Piero. Did Niccolò really leave his family "in direst poverty"? Was this unbeliever converted on his deathbed? "He allowed the rite of confession to be administered," Piero writes. This is not the place to decide which of his recent biographers is right: Russo, who claims that he was a Christian at heart; Ridolfi, who elevates him to sainthood – or close to it; Prezzolini, who baptizes him the antichrist. Here too, let us allow Machiavelli to speak for himself. And let us not merely listen to him; if we would seek the secret unity of so disparate a work, so rich a personality, let us harken to his own heartbeat. In his essay on Miachiavelli, Macaulay writes:

> Two characters altogether dissimilar are united in him. They are not merely joined, but interwoven. They are the warp and the woof of his mind; and their combination, like that of the variegated threads in shot silk, gives to the whole texture a glancing and ever-changing appearance.[1]

To this portrait let us add, in conclusion, the last lines of Machiavelli's portrait of Lorenzo the Magnificent: "There were in him two diverse beings, joined together with an invisible seam." Was Machiavelli perhaps thinking of himself when he penned these lines?

[1] *Critical and Historical Essays* (London, Longman, Brown, Green, and Longmans, 1854), Vol. I, p. 62.

ANTHOLOGY

THE CLIMATE OF THE TIMES

Florentine Comedy

MESSER NICIA: Tell me then; I will follow you in everything and trust you more than I do my confessor.

CALLIMACO: Then you must understand this: that there is nothing more certain to bring a woman to pregnancy than to give her a potion made from mandragola. It is an experiment I have made on several occasions and it has always succeeded; if it were not for this the queen of France would be childless, and so would innumerable other princesses in that land.

MESSER NICIA: Is it possible?

CALLIMACO: It is as I tell you. And fortune has favored you to such an extent that I have brought with me everything that the potion needs, and it can be yours whenever you wish.

MESSER NICIA: When should she take it?

CALLIMACO: This evening after dinner; the moon is in a favorable aspect and the time could not be more propitious.

MESSER NICIA: Don't worry about that. You just get it ready: I will see that she takes it.

CALLIMACO: However, one thing you must face: the man who first has to do with a woman who has taken this potion dies within eight days, and nothing in this world can save him.

MESSER NICIA: Death and damnation! I wouldn't touch the filthy stuff! You'll not play your tricks on me! A fine fix you'd be putting me in!

CALLIMACO: Keep calm; there is an alternative.

MESSER NICIA: Well, what is it?

CALLIMACO: To make someone else sleep with her. In a night he will have drawn off all the infection from the mandragola. Then you can resume your rights again without any danger.

MESSER NICIA: No, that I won't do.

CALLIMACO: Why not?

MESSER NICIA: Because I don't want to make my wife a whore and myself a cuckold.

CALLIMACO: Is that how you feel? I took you for a wiser man. So you hesitate to follow the King of France in this — and the whole of his court?

MESSER NICIA: But who do you think I could find to take part in such madness? If I tell him the truth, he will refuse; if I don't, I shall be deceiving him and putting a noose round my own neck. I don't want to look for trouble.

CALLIMACO: If that is all that worries you, leave everything to me.

MESSER NICIA: What will you do?

CALLIMACO: I will tell you. I will let you have the potion this evening after dinner; you give it her to drink, and put her straight to bed about four hours after dark. Then we shall disguise ourselves, you, Lugurio, Siro, and I, and we will scour the New Market and the Old Market, and the streets round here, and the first idle young lout we find, we'll throw a cloak over his head and whip him along in the dark into your house and up to your room. Then we will put him into bed, tell him what to do — and there won't be any difficulty at all. Afterwards, in the morning, pack him off before daybreak, get your wife to wash, and you can do what you like with her without the slightest danger.

MESSER NICIA: Well, since you say that the kings and princes and great lords have done the same, I am content. But, above all, as you value your life, let no one know of it!

CALLIMACO: Who do you think would tell?

MESSER NICIA: There is still one obstacle: and it's a tricky one.

CALLIMACO: What is that?

MESSER NICIA: To bring my wife round to it – and I can't believe that she would ever agree.

CALLIMACO: Very well then. But I should not pretend to the name of husband if I couldn't make my wife do as I wanted.

LIGURIO: I have thought of a way.

MESSER NICIA: How?

LIGURIO: Through her confessor.

CALLIMACO: But who will persuade the confessor?

LIGURIO: You, me, money, our baser selves – and his.

MESSER NICIA: None the less, I fear that if I suggest it, she will refuse to speak to her confessor.

LIGURIO: There's a remedy for that, too.

CALLIMACO: Tell me.

LIGURIO: Get her mother to take her to him.

MESSER NICIA: She certainly confides in her.

LIGURIO: And I know her mother will see things our way. Come now, we mustn't delay; it is getting late. You can go for a walk, Callimaco, but make sure that we find you at home with the potion ready two hours after nightfall. Messer Nicia and I will go to his mother-in-law's house to warn her; she and I understand one another. Then we will go to the friar, and we will let you know what happens.

(*Mandragola*, Act Two.)

LUCREZIA: This is what I have always been afraid of, that Messer Nicia's longing for an heir would make him do something outrageous; so I get anxious whenever he starts explaining some new idea – especially since you know what happened when I went to the Servites. But of all the ideas that he has had, this is the strangest. That I should have to be ravished, and that a man should die for having ravished me – If I were the only woman left in all the world, and responsible for replenishing the whole human race, I can't think I would be justified in doing this.

127

SOSTRATA: I haven't so many fine words, my girl. Talk to the friar, see what he has to say, and then do whatever you are advised by him, by us, and by all who love you.

LUCREZIA: Oh God, my heart is bursting. (*They go into the church.*)

FRA TIMOTEO: You are welcome. I know what you have come to see me about; Messer Nicia has spoken to me. To tell you the truth I have been poring over my books for hours, studying the case, and after careful research I find that there are numerous considerations on our side, both general and particular.

LUCREZIA: Do you mean it, or are you laughing at me?

FRA TIMOTEO: Ah, Madonna Lucrezia, is this a laughing matter? Am I such a stranger to you?

LUCREZIA: No, Father, but this is the most fantastic idea I ever heard.

FRA TIMOTEO: I believe you, madonna, but I do not want you to continue in this strain. There are many things which, afar off, seem strange, terrifying, intolerable, which when you come close appear natural, bearable, homely; because of this one says that fear of the evil is greater than the evil itself. And this is such a matter.

LUCREZIA: Please God it is.

FRA TIMOTEO: I want to go back to what I first said to you. As far as conscience is concerned, you have to accept this common rule: that where there is a certain good and an uncertain evil, the good must never be sacrificed for fear of the evil. Here we have a certain good – that you will conceive a child, gaining a soul for our Savior, Jesus Christ: the uncertain evil is that the man who shares your bed after you have taken the potion might die; but it may well turn out that he does not die. Nevertheless, as there is some doubt, it is better for Messer Nicia not to run any risk. As for the act itself, it is foolish to call that a sin, for it is the will that commits a sin, not the body; the real sin is to displease your husband, and you will be pleasing him; or to take pleasure in the act, and you will not take pleasure in it. Besides this, it is the outcome of any action that we have to bear in mind: the outcome of yours will be to content your husband and fill a place in Paradise. The Bible says that Lot's daughters, believing themselves left alone in the world, lay with their father; and, because their intention was good, they did not sin.

LUCREZIA: What advice do you give me then?

SOSTRATA: Just let yourself be advised, girl. Don't you realize that a childless wife is a homeless wife? When her husband is dead she is like a mere wild creature, abandoned by the world.

FRA TIMOTEO: I swear to you, madonna, by this sacred cloth that by obeying your husband in this matter your conscience will be no more burdened than if you were to eat meat on a Friday, and that is a sin which can be washed away with holy water.

LUCREZIA: Where are you leading me, Father?

FRA TIMOTEO: I am leading you to an action for which you will always want to pray God's blessing on me, and which will please you more in a year's time than it does now.

SOSTRATA: She will do what you wish. I am going to put her to bed myself. What are you frightened of, you silly girl? There are fifty women in this city who would give their eyes to be in your place.

LUCREZIA: Well, I consent – but I know I'll die before the morning comes.

FRA TIMOTEO: Have no fears, my child: I will pray God for you; I will intercede with the angel Raphael so that he will be with you. Go with God's blessing, and prepare yourself for the mystery, for it is already growing dark.

SOSTRATA: Peace be with you, Father.

LUCREZIA: God and Our Lady protect me and keep me from harm!

(*Mandragola*, Act III.)

Machiavelli has just learned that a conspiracy against the Emperor Charles V, which had been headed by the Duke of Milan and Morone, his secretary, and also involved Pope Clement VII and other rulers, has been found out and put down. At the same time, he learns that he is being given a larger "advance" on his History, and that there will shortly be a performance of his comedy. This is how he reported these events to his friend Guicciardini; note the signature.

. . . Morone has gotten caught and the Duchy of Milan is in a sad state: and just as the Duke got what was coming to him, so will the other princes; it is inevitable: *sic datum desuper.*

The fleur-de-lis is returning to Alagna
And in his Vicar [*etc.*]

Nosti versus caetera, per te ipsum lege.

Let's have a happy Carnival season for once; get la Barbera lodgings with the monks, and if they don't go out of their minds, I'll miss my guess. Give my regards to la Maliscotta, see how the plans for our comedy are going, and tell me when you are planning to put it on.

The advance I am to receive for the *History* has gone up to one hundred ducats. I am buckling down to writing again and am venting my spleen by attacking all those princes who have done everything they possibly could to get us in such a mess. *Valete.*

Niccolò Machiavelli
Historian, Comic Actor, Tragedian.
(*Familiar Letter 199*, dated October 20, 1525.)

Medici and Republicans

The Medici family did not ask of their historian that he preserve for posterity such of their Founding Father's remarks as these. The historian, however, believed in "telling the truth regardless."

[Cosimo de' Medici] was of ordinary stature, an olive complexion, and a venerable presence. Without erudition he was most eloquent, and abounded in natural good sense; he was, therefore, always obliging to his friends, compassionate to the poor, instructive in conversation, deliberate in council, rapid in execution, and in his sayings he was grave, in his repartees he was sarcastic. Not long after Rinaldo degli Albizzi was banished, he sent Cosimo word, "The hen was hatching." He returned the answer, that she would have but a bad hatching time, so far from the nest." And when some others of the exiles gave him to understand, "they were not asleep," he replied, "he thought he had spoiled their sleeping." He said of Pius, the Pontiff, when he was exciting the Christian princes to a crusade against the Turk, "that he was an old man, but his enterprise was worthy of a young one." When the ambassadors of the Venetians and of King Alphonso came to Florence to complain of the Republic, he

uncovered his head, and asked them to say what color it
bore. "White," they replied. "It will not be long," he added,
"before the heads of your Senators will be of the same color."
Not many hours before his death, his wife asked him, "why
he kept his eyes shut?" He told her, "it was to accustom them
to it." After his return from exile, some of the citizens
remonstrating "that the Republic would be weakened, and
God offended, by the expulsion of so many and such pious
men," he replied, "that an enfeebled Republic was better than
a Republic ruined; that a couple of ells of fine cloth made
many a one look like a good man; and that the power of
states was not maintained by Paternosters." (*The Florentine
Histories,* II.)

*He gave his friendship to those worthiest to receive it: to
the young people who gathered at the home of the Rucellai
in the Oricellari gardens. It was with them and for them
that he went back to Livy and, after a brief period of dis-
traction, really applied himself.*
He dedicated the result of his study and reflection, The
Discourses on the First Decade of Livy, *to Zanobi Buondel-
monti and Cosimo Rucellai.*

. . . I seem in this to be departing from the usual practice
of authors, which has always been to dedicate their works
to some prince, and, blinded by ambition and avarice, to
praise him for all his virtuous qualities when they ought
to have blamed him for all manner of shameful deeds.
So, to avoid this mistake, I have chosen not those who
are princes, but those who, on account of their innumerable
good qualities, deserve to be; not those who might shower
on me rank, honors, and riches, but those who, though
unable, would like to do so. . . . Entertain yourselves, then,
with what you were anxious to get, whether it be good or
bad; and, should you be so mistaken as to find my views
unacceptable, I shall not fail to follow this up with the rest
of the history as I promised at the start. (*The Discourses
of Niccolò Machiavelli,* I.)

Popes and Monks

It is revealing how Machiavelli mingles feelings of con-

Maximilien I.
à Spire en 1519, par Albert Dürer

tempt with those of wonderment when he considers the power and the historical durability of the religious institution.

"What a lot of things a pope can do!" observed Queen Christina of Sweden on the margins of this passage from The Prince.

OF ECCLESIASTICAL PRINCIPALITIES

It now only remains to us to speak of ecclesiastical principalities, with regard to which the difficulties lie wholly before they are possesed. They are acquired by ability (*virtù*) or by fortune; but are maintained without either, for they are sustained by ancient religious customs, which are so powerful and of such quality, that they keep their princes in power in whatever manner they proceed and live. These princes alone have states without defending them, have subjects without governing them, and their states, not being defended are not taken from them; their subjects not being governed do not resent it, and neither think nor are capable of alienating themselves from them. Only these principalities, therefore, are secure and happy. But as they are upheld by higher causes, which the human mind cannot attain to, I will abstain from speaking of them; for being exalted and maintained by God, it would be the work of a presumptuous and foolish man to discuss them.

. . . .

Then [after Alexander VI] came Pope Julius, who found the Church powerful, possessing all Romagna, all the Roman barons suppressed, and the factions destroyed by the severity of Alexander. He also found the way open for accumulating wealth in ways never used before the time of Alexander. These measures were not only followed by Julius, but increased; he resolved to gain Bologna, put down the Venetians and drive the French from Italy, in all which enterprises he was successful. He merits the greater praise, as he did everything to increase the power of the Church and not of any private person. (*The Prince*, Chapter XI.)

Many people succeed in their designs by weighing and measuring everything. This present Pope has no scale or gauge to his name; but, acting aimlessly and unarmed, he

133

Maximilian I. "This great, bony, thoroughly military face with a monumental nose is a Don Quixote without naiveté" (Michelet)

succeeds in doing things that he could hardly do with the best laid plans and the most efficient weapons. (*Familiar Letter* 116 to Piero Soderini, September, 1512.)

This is how Machiavelli saw through Savonarola's oratory and, after four years of theocratic dictatorship, unmasked the Friar's pretense of being above all factions:

... when you hear how boldly he began to preach there, and is continuing to preach, you will probably be not a little surprised. He was in the greatest alarm as to his own safety, that the new Government was resolved out of hand to destroy him. He knew, however, that many people in Florence would be involved in his ruin; so he began with terrifying horrors, showing with arguments that must have been very effective with people not trained to thinking, that his followers were very fine people while his opponents were the worst sort of rascals. He went to any limit that seemed likely to weaken the hostile party and strengthen his own. I must tell you briefly of some of the things he said, since I was present and heard them. ...

Later on, however, the Government wrote to the Pope in the Friar's favor, and the Friar could see that he had nothing more to fear from his enemies in Florence. At first he tried to hold his party together by vituperating his antagonists and fighting them by calling them tyrants. Now he sees that he no longer needs to do this and is changing tack. Still urging his followers to stand together as at first, he has stopped talking of tyrants and their wickedness and is trying to rouse everybody against the Pope; and in turning his fire upon the Pontiff he is saying of him things you might say of the worst rascal you can think of. So, as I see it, he goes on taking advantage of the moment and adapting his slanders to circumstances. (Letter from Machiavelli to Ricciardo Bechi, March 9, 1498 [dated 1497].)

To his prince, Machiavelli counseled the very deception he disapproved of in the monk – on the condition that it be skillfully dissembled.

Here, however, he acknowledges another "monkery" besides that of the humbugs, the charlatans, and the politicians who wore the habit. While he did not himself share the faith of St. Francis of Assisi, he respected it and declared, moreover, that it is necessary to the State.

As to religious institutions one sees here again how necessary these renovations are from the example of our own religion, which, if it had not been restored to its starting-point by St. Francis and St. Dominic, would have become quite extinct. For these men by their poverty and by their exemplification of the life of Christ revived religion in the minds of men in whom it was already dead, and so powerful were these new religious orders that they prevented the depravity of prelates and of religious heads from bringing ruin on religion. They also lived so frugally and had such prestige with the populace as confessors and preachers that they convinced them it is an evil thing to talk evilly of evil doing, and a good thing to live under obedience to such prelates, and that, if they did wrong, it must be left to God to chastise them. And, this being so, the latter behave as badly as they can, because they are not afraid of punishments which they do not see and in which they do not believe. It is, then, this revival which has maintained and continues to maintain this religion. (*Discourses, III,* i.)

The Map of Europe

Machiavelli caught glimpses of Tacitus' Germany in Switzerland and the Tyrol and after laying bare the grandeur and the wretchedness of the Holy Roman Empire and its sixteenth-century leader, he concluded: "This is why Germany's power is great, but great in a way that is useless to everyone else." The following sketch of Emperor Maximilian, "the greatest of the Hapsburgs" (according to Renaudet), must certainly have served Michelet for the full-length portrait he drew in his History of France.

Having written on my return here last year all I knew about the affairs of Germany and the Emperor, I am really at a loss as to what more to say on the subject. I shall confine myself therefore to a few remarks about the character of the Emperor. There is not, and perhaps never has been, a prince more wasteful than he is. This is the reason why he is always in want, and why he never has money enough, no matter in what situation he may find himself.

He is very fickle, wanting one thing to-day, and next day caring nothing about it; he takes counsel from no one, and yet believes everybody. He desires what he cannot have, and leaves that which he can readily obtain; and therefore he always takes contradictory solutions.

On the other hand he is most warlike, and knows how to maintain and conduct an army well, preserving justice and discipline. He bears any kind of fatigue as well as any other man inured to it; is courageous in danger, and as a general is not inferior to any man of the present day. He is affable in his audiences, but will grant them only when it suits him; he does not like ambassadors to come and pay their court to him, unless he sends for them; he is extremely reticent; he lives in a constant state of agitation of mind and body, and often undoes in the evening what he has concluded in the morning. This makes the missions near him very difficult..... (*Discourse on the Affairs of Germany and On the Emperor* [1509].)

That Machiavelli did not care for France or for the French is by no means sure, when all his references are taken into account. But however he may personally have felt, as an observer he never failed to pay his respects to the unity of the nation, to its wealth, to its balance of powers within the hierarchical structure, where "gentlemen give orders to the common people, where princes give orders to gentlemen, and the king to princes."

By the extent of her territory and the advantages derived from her large rivers, France is very productive and opulent; but the abundant productions of the soil, as well as manual labor, have little or no value, owing to the scarcity of money amongst the people, who can scarcely get enough together to pay their dues to the lord proprietor, although the amounts are but very small. This arises from their not having an outlet for the productions of the soil, for every man gathers enough to sell some; so that if in any one place a man wanted to sell a bushel of grain, he would not find a purchaser, everybody having grain to sell. And of the money which the gentlemen draw from their tenants, they spend nothing except for their clothing; for they have cattle enough to give them meat, innumerable fowls, lakes full of fish, and parks with an abundance of every variety of game;

and thus almost every gentleman lives upon his estates. In this way all the money accumulates in the hands of the proprietors, and their wealth is accordingly great; whilst the people, when they have a florin, deem themselves rich.

The prelates of France draw two fifths of their revenues and wealth from the kingdom, there being a good many bishoprics having incomes from temporal as well as spiritual sources. And as they have abundant supplies of all the necessaries of life, all the revenues and moneys that come into their hands never leave them again, according to the avaricious nature of prelates and churchmen; and all the money that is collected by the chapters and colleges of the Church is spent for silver, jewels, and costly church ornaments. Thus the Church properties and what the prelates possess privately in the way of money and silver plate, etc., amount to an immense treasure. . . .

The Frenchman is naturally covetous of other people's goods, of which, together with his own, he is afterwards prodigal. Thus, the Frenchman will rob most skilfully, to eat, or to waste what he has robbed, or even to enjoy it together with the very person whom he has robbed; entirely different from the Spaniard, who will never let you see again what he has taken from you. . . .

The French people are submissive and most obedient, and hold their king in great veneration. They live at a very small expense, owing to the great abundance of the products of the soil; and every one has a small property to himself. They live at a very small expense, owing to the great abundance of the products of the soil; and every one has a small property to himself. They dress coarsely, in cheap cloth, and neither the men nor the women use silk in any way, for it would at once be noted by the gentlemen. (*An Account of the Affairs of France.*)

Among the kingdoms that are well ordered and governed in our time is France, and there we find numberless good institutions on which depend the liberty and security of the king; of these the chief is the parliament and its authority, because he who established that kingdom, knowing the ambition and insolence of the great nobles, deemed it necessary to have a bit in their mouths to check them. And knowing on the other hand the hatred of the mass of the people against the great, based on fear, and wishing to secure them, he did not wish to make this the special care of the king, to relieve him of the dissatisfaction that he might incur among the nobles by favouring the people, and among the people by favouring the nobles. He therefore established a third judge that, without direct charge of the king, kept in check the great and favoured the lesser people. Nor could any better or more prudent measure have been adopted, nor better precaution for the safety of the king and the kingdom. From which another notable rule can be drawn, that princes should let the carrying out of unpopular duties devolve on others, and bestow favours themselves. I conclude again by saying that a prince must esteem his nobles, but not make himself hated by the populace. (*The Prince*, Chapter XIX.)

Ambitions for Italy

It is a contradiction, but a very human one, that Machiavelli dreamed of the unification of Italy long before that dream became a reality, and yet did not urge the adoption of a single Italian dialect, common to the whole peninsula. An even more striking contradiction is illustrated in the following passage, in which Machiavelli (who said that it is "evil not to call evil by its right name") criticizes Dante for having said exactly what he thought of his native city.

But I shall say no more of Dante, whose genius, teachings, and judgment all proved that he was a great man, except when he spoke on the subject of his native city, which he attacked on every possible occasion, with a passion unworthy of a philosopher or a man. He could not resist vilifying it; he accused it of every possible vice; he condemned its inhabitants; he criticized the way it had been built; he spoke ill of its customs and the laws which govern it. He does not take this tone in just one canto of his poem; it runs through the whole work, being expressed in many ways and numerous figures of speech; for the injustice of his exile had cut him to the quick and he wanted vengeance with all his heart. He wreaked the most terrible vengeance that he could; and if fate had decreed that a single one of the evils that he called down upon his native city had really befallen Florence, the grief of having nurtured such a man would have made her suffer more than any of the other ills that overtook her. But Fortune, as if to give the lie to him and shroud the poet's calumnies in clouds of glory, has ever caused Florence to flourish; She has caused Florence's glory to be recognized in every corner of the earth; and She has brought the city such great blessings, so deep a peace, that if Dante were resurrected so that he might see Florence once again, he would be so overwhelmed at this frustration of his incorrigible malice that he would either confess his error, or seek to die a second time. *(Discourse on Language.)*

How could anyone so firmly convinced of the gullibility of some people and the ability of others to outwit their fellows to their own ends address so high-minded an appeal to a member of the Medici clan, about whom he has no illusions whatsoever? How could anyone speak of a united Italy to princes concerned only with their own dynastic ambitions? It is astonishing, but this is the tenor of the entire last chapter of Machiavelli's "Breviary for Tyrants." Edgar Quinet said of this passage: "It is a sixteenth-century national anthem, a clarion call to the future ... in which the writer takes off his mask and reveals himself in his true colors ... no wolf in sheep's clothing, but a lion merely pretending to be a fox."

Having now considered all the things we have spoken of, and thought within myself whether at present the time was not propitious in Italy for a new prince, and if there was not a state of things which offered an opportunity to a prudent and capable man to introduce a new system that would do honour to himself and good to the mass of the people, it seems to me that so many things concur to favour a new ruler that I do not know of any time more fitting for such an enterprise. And if, as I said, it was necessary in order that the power of Moses should be displayed that the people of Israel should be slaves in Egypt, and to give scope for the greatness and courage of Cyrus that the Persians should be oppressed by the Medes, and to illustrate the pre-eminence of Theseus that the Athenians should be dispersed, so at the present time, in order that the might of an Italian genius might be recognised, it was necessary that Italy should be reduced to her present condition, and that she

139

should be more enslaved than the Hebrews, more oppressed than the Persians, and more scattered than the Athenians; without a head, without order, beaten, despoiled, lacerated and overrun, and that she should have suffered ruin of every kind.

And although before now a gleam of hope has appeared which gave hope that some individual might be appointed by God for her redemption, yet at the highest summit of his career he was thrown aside by fortune, so that now, almost lifeless, she awaits one who may heal her wounds and put a stop to the pillaging of Lombardy, to the rapacity and extortion in the Kingdom of Naples and in Tuscany, and cure her of those sores which have long been festering. Behold how she prays God to send some one to redeem her from this barbarous cruelty and insolence. Behold her ready and willing to follow any standard if only there be some one to raise it. . . .

If your illustrious house, therefore, wishes to follow those great men who redeemed their countries, it is before all things necessary, as the true foundation of every undertaking, to provide yourself with your own forces, for you cannot have more faithful, or truer and better soldiers. And although each one of them may be good, they will united become even better when they see themselves commanded by their prince, and honoured and favoured by him. It is therefore necessary to prepare such forces in order to be able with Italian prowess to defend the country from foreigners. And although both the Swiss and Spanish infantry are deemed terrible, none the less they each have their defects, so that a third method of array might not only oppose them, but be confident of overcoming them. For the Spaniards cannot sustain the attack of cavalry, and the Swiss have to fear infantry which meets them with resolution equal to their own. From which it has resulted, as will be seen by experience, that the Spaniards cannot sustain the attack of French cavalry, and the Swiss are overthrown by Spanish infantry. And although a complete example of the latter has not been seen, yet an instance was furnished in the battle of Ravenna, where the Spanish infantry attacked the German battalions, which are organized in the same way as the Swiss. The Spaniards, through their bodily agility and aided by their bucklers, had entered between and under their pikes and were in a position to attack them safely without the Germans being able to defend themselves; and if the cavalry had not charged them they would have utterly destroyed them. Knowing therefore the defects of both these kinds of infantry, a third kind can be created which can resist cavalry and need not fear infantry, and this will be done by the choice of arms and a new organisation. And these are the things which, when newly introduced, give reputation and grandeur to a new prince.

This opportunity must not, therefore, be allowed to pass, so that Italy may at length find her liberator. I cannot express the love with which he would be received in all those provinces which have suffered under these foreign invasions, with what thirst for vengeance, with what steadfast faith, with what love, with what grateful tears. What doors would be closed against him? What people would refuse him obedience? What envy could oppose him? What Italian would withhold allegiance? This barbarous domination stinks in the nostrils of everyone. May your illustrious house therefore assume this task with that courage and those hopes which are inspired by a just cause, so that under its banner our fatherland may be raised up, and under its auspices be verified that saying of Petrarch:

> Valour against fell wrath
> Will take up arms; and be the combat quickly sped!
> For, sure, the ancient worth,
> That in Italians stirs the heart, is not yet dead.

(The Prince, Chapter XXVII.)

CIVITASARETII

"LA VERITA EFFETTUALE DELLE COSE"

"The hypothesis of the Prince"

In his reports to the Ten early in his career, Machiavelli had already formed the habit of taking crisp notes and making detached comments on the events he witnessed and the men responsible for them. In Chapter VII of The Prince, *written ten years after the events here described, he turns a not very complicated, but violent and tragic instance of papal nepotism into what the French historian Renaudet called "the Dantean myth of the National Savior."*

Cesare Borgia, commonly called Duke Valentine, acquired the state by the influence of his father and lost it when that influence failed, and that although every measure was adopted by him and everything done that a prudent and capable man could do to establish himself firmly in a state that the arms and the favours of others had given him. For, as we have said, he who does not lay his foundations beforehand may by great abilities do so afterwards, although with great trouble to the architect and danger to the building. If, then, one considers the procedure of the duke, it will be seen how firm were the foundations he had laid to his

143

future power, which I do not think it superfluous to examine, as I know of no better precepts for a new prince to follow than may be found in his actions; and if his measures were not successful, it was through no fault of his own but only by the most extraordinary malignity of fortune. . . .

. . . the Orsini seeing at length that the greatness of the duke and of the Church meant their own ruin, convoked a diet at Magione in the Perugino. Hence sprang the rebellion of Urbino and the tumults in Romagna and infinite dangers to the duke, who overcame them all with the help of the French; and having regained his reputation, neither trusting France nor other foreign forces, in order not to venture on their alliance, he had recourse to stratagem. He dissembled his aims so well that the Orsini made their peace with him, being represented by Signor Paolo whose suspicions the duke disarmed with every courtesy, presenting him with robes, money, and horses, so that in their simplicity they were induced to come to Sinigaglia and fell into his hands. Having thus suppressed these leaders and made their partisans his friends, the duke had laid a very good foundation to his power, having all the Romagna with the duchy of Urbino, and having gained the favour of the inhabitants, who began to feel the benefit of his rule.

And as this part is worthy of note and of imitation by others, I will not omit mention of it. When he took the Romagna, it had previously been governed by weak rulers, who had rather despoiled their subjects than governed them, and given them more cause for disunion than for union, so that the province was a prey to robbery, assaults, and every kind of disorder. He, therefore, judged it necessary to give them a good government in order to make them peaceful and obedient to his rule. For this purpose he appointed Messer Remirro de Orco, a cruel and able man, to whom he gave the fullest authority. This man, in a short time, was highly successful in rendering the country orderly and united, whereupon the duke, not deeming such excessive authority expedient, lest it should become hateful, appointed a civil court of justice in the centre of the province under an excellent president, to which each city appointed its own advocate. And as he knew that the harshness of the past had engendered some amount of hatred, in order to purge the minds of the people and to win them over completely, he resolved to show that if any cruelty had taken place it was not by his orders, but through the harsh disposition of his minister. And having found the opportunity he had him cut in half and placed one morning in the public square at Cesena with a piece of wood and blood-stained knife by his side. The ferocity of this spectacle caused the people both satisfaction and amazement. But to return to where we left off.

The duke being now powerful and partly secured against present perils, being armed himself, and having in a great measure put down those neighbouring forces which might injure him, had now to get the respect of France, if he wished to proceed with his acquisitions, for he knew that the king, who had lately discovered his error, would not give him any help. He began therefore to seek fresh alliances and to vacillate with France on the occasion of the expedition that the French were undertaking towards the kingdom of Naples against the Spaniards, who were besieging Gaeta. His intention was to assure himself of them, which he would soon have succeeded in doing if Alexander had lived.

These were the measures taken by him with regard to the present. As to the future, he feared that a new successor to the states of the Church might not be friendly to him and might seek to deprive him of what Alexander had given him, and he sought to provide against this in four ways. First, by destroying all who were of the blood of those ruling families which he had despoiled, in order to deprive the pope of any opportunity. Secondly, by gaining the friendship of the Roman nobles, so that he might through them hold as it were the pope in check. Thirdly, by obtaining as great a hold on the College as he could. Fourthly, by acquiring such power before the pope died as to be able to resist alone the first onslaught. Of these four things he had at the death of Alexander accomplished three, and the fourth he had almost accomplished. For of the dispossessed rulers he killed as many as he could lay hands on, and very few escaped; he had gained to his party the Roman nobles; and he had a great influence in the College. As to the new possessions, he designed to become lord of Tuscany, and already possessed Perugia and Piombino, and has assumed the protectorate over Pisa; and as he had no longer to fear the French (for the French had been deprived of the king-

145

dom of Naples by the Spaniards in such a way that both parties were obliged to buy his friendship) he seized Pisa. After this, Lucca and Siena at once yielded, partly through hate of the Florentines and partly through fear; the Florentines had no resources, so that, had he succeeded as he had done before, in the very year that Alexander died he would have gained such strength and renown as to be able to maintain himself without depending on the fortunes or strength of others, but solely by his own power and ability. But Alexander died five years after Cesare Borgia had first drawn his sword. He was left with only the state of Romagna firmly established, and all the other schemes in mid-air, between two very powerful and hostile armies, and suffering from a fatal illness. But the valour and ability of the duke were such, and he knew so well how to win over men or vanquish them, and so strong were the foundations that he had laid in this short time, that if he had not had those two armies upon him, or else had been in good health, he would have survived every difficulty. And that his foundations were good is seen from the fact that the Romagna waited for him more than a month; in Rome, although half dead, he remained secure, and although the Baglioni, Vitelli, and Orsini entered Rome they found no followers against him. He was able, if not to make pope whom he wished, at any rate to prevent a pope being created whom he did not wish. But if at the death of Alexander he had been well, everything would have been easy. And he told me on the day that Pope Julius II was elected, that he had thought of everything which might happen on the death of his father, and provided against everything, except that he had never thought that at his father's death he would be dying himself.

Reviewing thus all the actions of the duke, I find nothing to blame, on the contrary, I feel bound, as I have done, to hold him up as an example to be imitated by all who by fortune and with the arms of others have risen to power. For with his great courage and high ambition he could not have acted otherwise, and his designs were only frustrated by the short life of Alexander and his own illness. Whoever, therefore, deems it necessary in his new principality to secure himself against enemies, to gain friends, to conquer by force or fraud, to make himself beloved and feared by the people, followed and reverenced by the soldiers, to destroy those who can and may injure him, introduce innovations into old customs, to be severe and kind, magnanimous and liberal, suppress the old militia, create a new one, maintain the friendship of kings and princes in such a way that they are glad to benefit him and fear to injure him, such a one can find no better example than the actions of this man. The only thing he can be accused of is that in the creation of Julius II he made a bad choice, for, as has been said, not being able to choose his own pope, he could still prevent any one individual being made pope, and he ought never to have permitted any of those cardinals to be raised to the papacy whom he had injured, or who when pope would stand in fear of him. For men commit injuries either through fear or through hate. Those whom he had injured were, among others, San Pietro ad Vincula, Colonna, San Giorgio, and Ascanio. All the others, if elected to the pontificate, would have had to fear him except Rohan and the Spaniards; the latter through their relationship and obligations to him, the former from his great power, being related to the King of France. For these reasons the duke ought above all things to have created a Spaniard pope; and if unable, then he should have consented to Rohan being appointed and not San Pietra ad Vincula. And whoever thinks that in high personages new benefits cause old offences to be forgotten, makes a great mistake. The duke, therefore, erred in this choice, and it was the cause of his ultimate ruin. (*The Prince*, Chapter VII.)

Machiavelli was no less divided in his mind about Pope Julius II than about Cesare Borgia. Although he admired – afterward – the man who dreamed of liberating Italy, he was as hostile as Dante had been to the incursions of the Spiritual Power in the sphere of the Temporal. He found the Princes of the Church just as double-faced as the secular princes.

VERY RARELY DO MEN KNOW HOW TO BE EITHER WHOLLY GOOD OR WHOLLY BAD

Pope Julius II, on going to Bologna in 1505 to expel from that state the house of Bentivogli, who had held that city as a principality for a hundred years, resolved also to remove Giovampagolo Baglioni from Perugia, where he was

147

ruling as a tyrant, for the pope had sworn to be rid of all tyrants who had seized the estates of the Church. Being thus minded and for this purpose, as everyone knew, he hurried to Perugia and did not wait for the army which was to protect him before entering the city, but entered it unarmed, in spite of the fact that Giovampagolo was there in person with a strong body of troops which he had collected for his defense. Carried away by that impetuosity which characterised all his actions, he thus placed himself and the simple guard he had with him in the hands of his enemy; yet took his enemy away with him, and left in the city a governor who should be responsible to the Church.

Prudent men who were with the pope were astonished at the pope's rashness and at the cowardice displayed by Giovampagolo; nor could they understand how it came about that the latter did not acquire perpetual fame by getting rid of his enemy at a single stroke and enriching himself with the booty; for with the pope were all the cardinals in all their splendor. They could not believe that it was any good motive, or his conscience, that held him back, for the heart of a criminal who had committed incest with his own sister and to gain the throne had put to death his cousins and his nephews, could scarce be influenced by any pious consideration. So they concluded it must be due to men not knowing how to be either magnificently bad or perfectly good; and that since evil deeds have a certain grandeur and are openhanded in their way, Giovampagolo was incapable of performing them.

Thus Giovampagolo, who thought nothing of incest or of publicly murdering his relatives, knew not how, or better, did not dare, to avail himself of an excellent opportunity to do what would have caused everyone to admire his courage and would have gained for him immortal fame, since he would have been the first to show prelates how little men are respected who live and rule as they do, and would have done a thing the greatness of which would have obliterated any infamy and any danger that might arise from it. (*Discourses, I*, xxvii.)

The Most Sublime Perfidy

There are several versions of the text which follows.
When Machiavelli learned that his first account of the
ambush at Sinigaglia had not been received by Their Mag-
nificences – about the worst fate that can befall a reporter –
he began a new account, some days later, which was never
finished. This letter begins as follows:

Magnificent Signori, etc.
As your Lordships have not received all my letters, which
would in great part have informed you of the circumstances
connected with the event that has taken place at Sinigaglia,
I think it proper to give you by the present full particulars
of the same. I have ample leisure to do so now, having
intrusted to our magnificent ambassador all the business
we have to attend to here at present. And I believe that it
will be agreeable to you to know these details, on account
of the character of the event, which is in all respects remark-
able and memorable.... *(Official Letter LIII to the Ten.)*

A third version of the episode was written in March,
1503, under the title: Description of the Manner in which
the Duke Valentine Proceeded to Kill Vitellozzo Vitelli,
Oliverotto da Fermo, and the Signor Pagolo and the Duke
Gravina Orsini. A comparison of the variants proves that
time and aesthetic considerations led Machiavelli to retouch
the strict truth.

... But the Duke did not for a moment stop his preparations, and made every effort to increase both his infantry
and his mounted force; and to prevent these preparations
from being noticed, he distributed his troops separately
through all the places of the Romagna. Meantime some
five hundred French lances had come to him, and although
he felt strong enough to revenge himself upon his enemies
by open war, yet he thought it would be safer and more
advantageous for him to keep up his deception, and not to
stop his peace negotiations. And so well did he manage this
matter, that he concluded a peace with them, according to
which he confirmed to each of them their old engagements;
he paid them four thousand ducats at once, and promised
them not to disturb the Bentivogli. He also concluded a

149

matrimonial alliance with Giovanni, and consented that none of them should ever be constrained to appear in person before him, except so far as it might suit themselves to do so. On the other hand, they promised to restore the duchy of Urbino to him, as well as all the other places which they had taken up to that day, to serve him in all his expeditions, and not to make war upon any one without his permission, nor to engage themselves in the service of any one else.

After the conclusion of this treaty, Guido Ubaldo, Duke of Urbino, fled again to Venice, having first caused all the fortresses in his state to be dismantled; for having full confidence in the population, he did not want these fortresses, which he believed he could not defend, to fall into the enemy's hands, who might use them to restrain and oppress

his friends. But the Duke Valentino, after having concluded this convention, and having distributed all his troops and the French lances throughout the Romagna, suddenly left Imola, about the end of November, and went to Cesena, where he remained many days, negotiating with the agents of the Vitelli and the Orsini, who happened to be with their troops in the duchy of Urbino, as to what new enterprises were to be undertaken. But as nothing was concluded, Oliverotto da Fermo was sent to make him the offer, that, if he were disposed to undertake the conquest of Tuscany, they were ready to cooperate with him; but if not, then they would go and endeavor to capture Sinigaglia. To which the Duke replied, that he had no intention of carrying the war into Tuscany, as the Florentines were his friends; but that he should be well pleased that they should take Sinigaglia.

Very soon after that, news came that the place had capitulated, but that the citadel had refused to surrender to them, the governor being unwilling to give it up to any one except to the Duke in person; and therefore they urged him to come there at once. The opportunity seemed favorable to the Duke, and his going not likely to give umbrage, as he had been called by them, and did not go of his own accord. And to make things the more sure, he dismissed all the French troops, who returned to Lombardy, except the one hundred lances under the command of Monseigneur de Caudales, his brother-in-law; and having left Cesena about the middle of December, he went on to Fano. There he employed all the cunning and sagacity that he was capable of; he persuaded Vitelli and the Orsini to await him at Sinigaglia, assuring them that mistrust could not make the agreement between them more sincere nor more durable, and that, so far as he was concerned, he only wanted to be able to avail himself of the arms and advice of his friends. And although Vitellozzo remained very reluctant to accept the invitation, his brother's death having taught him that a prince whom you have once offended is not to be trusted, yet he yielded to the persuasion of Pagolo Orsino, who had been corrupted by presents and promises of the Duke to wait for him at Sinigaglia. The Duke thereupon, before leaving for Fano, on the 30th of December, communicated his plan to eight of his most trusty followers, amongst whom were Don Michele and Monseigneur d'Enna, who afterwards became Cardinal. He directed them that so soon as Vitellozzo, Pagolo Orsino, the Duke Gravina, and Oliverotto came to meet him, each two of them should take one of these four between them; they were to entertain them until their arrival at Sinigaglia, and were not to permit them to leave until they had reached the Duke's lodgings, where they were to make them prisoners. After that he ordered that all his armed force, consisting of more than two thousand horse and ten thousand infantry, should be at the break of day on the Metauro, a river five miles from Fano, and there to wait for him. Having met them there on the morning of the last day of December, he sent about two hundred of his mounted men ahead toward Sinigaglia, and then he started his infantry, after which he came himself with the remainder of his mounted force. . . .

The Vitelli and the Orsini, having given orders to await

the coming of the Duke, had, by way of personally showing
him honor, and for the purpose of lodging his troops, sent
their own away to some castles about six miles distant from
Sinigaglia, and had only left Oliverotto with his men in
Sinigaglia; these consisted of one thousand infantry and one
hundred and fifty mounted men, who were quartered in the
above-mentioned suburb. Matters being thus arranged, the
Duke Valentino went towards Sinigaglia; and when the head
of his cavalry had reached the bridge, they did not pass it,
but halted, and one half faced the river, and the other half
fronted towards the country, leaving a space between them
for the infantry to pass through, who entered the place
without halting. Vitellozzo, Pagolo and the Duke Gravina,
mounted on mules, and accompanied by a few horsemen,
came to meet the Duke. Vitellozzo was without arms, and
wore a cloak lined with green; he seemed very sad, as though
he had a presentiment of the death that awaited him, which
caused some astonishment, as his valor and former fortune
were well known. It was said that, when he parted from his
troops to come to Sinigaglia for the purpose of meeting the
Duke, it seemed as though he bade them goodby forever.
He recommended his house and fortune to his captains, and
admonished his nephews not to remember the fortune of their
house, but only the valor of their fathers.

When the three arrived before the Duke, they saluted
him courteously, and were graciously received by him; and
those to whom the Duke had committed their charge took
them at once between them. But when the Duke noticed
that Oliverotto was not with them (he having remained with
his troops at Sinigaglia, whom the kept arrayed in line in the
square opposite his lodgings by the river, where he made
them go through their exercises), he gave a wink to Don
Michele, to whose charge Oliverotto had been confided, to
see that Oliverotto should not escape. Don Michele there
rode ahead, and having found Oliverotto he told him that
this was not the time to keep the troops out of their quarters, which might otherwise be taken from them by the
troops of the Duke; and therefore he advised him to let the
troops go into their quarters, and come himself with him to
meet the Duke. Oliverotto followed this advice, and went
to join the Duke, who so soon as he saw him called him;
and after having duly saluted the Duke, he joined the
others.

Georges, Cardinal d'Amboise, known in Machiavelli's day as "Rohan"

When they had entered Sinigaglia they all dismounted at the Duke's lodgings, and, having entered with him into an inner chamber, they were all made prisoners. The Duke immediately mounted his horse and ordered the troops of Oliverotto and the Orsini to be disarmed and stripped. Oliverotto's troops, being near by, were completely stripped, but those of the Vitelli and the Orsini, being at a distance and having apprehended the destruction of their masters, had time to unite, and, recalling the valor and discipline of the Orsini and the Vitelli, drew together, and succeeded in saving themselves despite of the efforts of the people of the country and the hostile troops. The Duke's soliders, not satisfied with plundering the troops of Oliverotto, began to sack Sinigaglia, and they would have completely pillaged the town, if the Duke had not repressed their rapacity by having a number of them put to death.

But when night came and the disturbances were stopped, the Duke thought it time to make away with Vitellozzo and Oliverotto; and having them both brought into the same chamber, he had them strangled. Neither of them before death said a single word worthy of their past lives. Vitellozzo conjured those who put him to death to implore the Pope to grant him a plenary indulgence for all his crimes. Oliverotto, weeping, cast all the blame for the injuries done the Duke upon Vitellozzo. Pagolo and the Duke Gravina Orsini were left alive until Duke Valentino heard that the Pope had seized the Cardinal Orsino, the Archbishop of Florence, and Messer Jacopo da Santa Croce. After having received this intelligence, the Signor Pagolo and the Duke Gravina were strangled in the same way as the others, at Castel della Pieve, on the 18th of January, 1503.

Explanations

King Louis was called into Italy by the ambition of the Venetians, who wished by his coming to gain half of Lombardy. I will not blame the king for coming nor for the part he took, because wishing to plant his foot in Italy, and not having friends in the country, on the contrary the conduct of King Charles having caused all doors to be closed to him, he was forced to accept what friendships he could find, and his schemes would have speedily been successful if he had made no mistakes in his others proceedings. . . .

Consider how little difficulty the king would have had in maintaining his reputation in Italy if he had observed the aforesaid rules, and kept a firm and sure hold over all those friends of his, who being many in number and weak, and fearful, one of the Church, another of the Venetians, were always obliged to hold fast to him, and by whose aid he could easily make sure of any who were still great. But he was hardly in Milan before he did exactly the opposite, by giving aid to Pope Alexander to occupy the Romagna. Nor did he perceive that, in taking this course, he weakened himself, by casting off his friends and those who had fled to his protection, and strengthened the Church by adding further temporal powers to the spiritual power, which gives it such authority. And having made the first mistake, he was obliged to follow it up, whilst, to put a stop to the ambition of Alexander and prevent him becoming ruler of Tuscany, he was forced to come to Italy. And not content with having increased the power of the Church and lost his friends, he now coveting the kingdom of Naples, divided it with the king of Spain; and where he alone was the arbiter of Italy, he now brought in a companion, so that the ambitious of that province who were dissatisfied with him might have some one else to appeal to; and where he might have left in that kingdom a king tributary to himself, he dispossessed him in order to bring in another who was capable of driving him out.

The desire to acquire possessions is a very natural and ordinary thing, and when those men do it who can do so successfully, they are always praised and not blamed, but when they cannot and yet want to do so at all costs, they make a mistake deserving of great blame. If France, therefore, with her own forces could have taken Naples, she ought to have done so; if she could not, she ought not to have shared it. And if the partition of Lombardy with the Venetians is to be excused, as having been the means of allowing the French king to set foot in Italy, this other partition deserves blame, not having the excuse of necessity.

Louis had thus made these five mistakes: he had crushed the smaller Powers, increased the power in Italy of one potentate, brought into the land a very powerful foreigner, he had not come to live there himself, nor had he established any colonies. . . .

Thus King Louis lost Lombardy through not observing any of those conditions which have been observed by others who have taken provinces and wished to retain them. Nor is this any miracle, but very reasonable and natural. I spoke of this matter with Cardinal Rohan at Nantes when Valentine, as Cesare Borgia, son of Pope Alexander, was commonly called, was occupying the Romagna, for on Cardinal Rohan saying to me that the Italians did not understand war, I replied that the French did not understand politics, for if they did they would never allow the Church to become so great. And experience shows us that the greatness in Italy of the Church and also of Spain have been caused by France, and her ruin has proceeded from them. From which may be drawn a general rule, which never or very rarely fails, that whoever is the cause of another becoming powerful, is ruined himself; for that power is produced by him either through craft or force; and both of these are suspected by the one who has been raised to power. (*The Prince,* Chapter III.)

In the following passage Machiavelli is no longer deploying tin soldiers or calculating the cost of fortifications. He is casting an eye at the map and considering the matter of invasion routes through the Apennines – roads he himself had traveled more than a few times in the course of his efforts to keep the peace.

On the other hand, the shortest road is the one of Sasso, but it is regarded by those who know the country well to be the most difficult, and the Signor Federigo da Bozzolo expresses the same opinion of it in a letter written by him to the Lord Lieutenant; and I believe that they know very well, that both on this side and towards Florence the road has been cut and fortified, so as to render it still more difficult. To come by the Alps of Crespino or San Benedetto seems to us out of all reason, so that we doubt much whether they would not have to turn back and descend into the Lucchese territory by the Garfagnana, which amongst all these difficult routes is the easiest; and once having passed it, they would find inhabitants who would furnish them supplies, but would not combat them.

The road by the Marecchia, and passing the Borgo a San Sepolcro, respecting which it seems there are some fears, is easier than that of the Garfagnana, but is much less convenient than what is believed here; and for that reason it would be easier for them to fall back three days' march, so as to enter the Lucchese territory promptly, where they would be received with open arms, instead of having to march six or eight days through the enemy's territory, where they would be obliged to fight their way through from the beginning.

There is another route which has come into notice within

the past few days, respecting which, however, there are great doubts; it begins below Bologna four miles in the direction of Imola; it crosses the Iddice and brings up at Cavrenno and at Pietramala, and runs from there along the Stale to Barberino. This was the route which the Duke Valentino took when he attacked Florence in 1501, and is considered much less wild than that of the Sasso. There is a messenger here sent by the inhabitants of Firenzuola to learn what measures are to be taken in case our troops should move in that direction; the Lord Lieutenant has conferred with this person about that road, and has learned the same thing from him. True, he says that about four miles from Stale there is a place called Covigliano, where there is a bad pass that can be made even worse; and about a mile from there is another pass called Castro, which is difficult by nature, but can be made still more so.... (Bologna, 12 March, 1527. *Official Letter 9* from Machiavelli to the Eight.)

Complaints

Note the modesty with which Machiavelli submits his petition and how he apologizes for demanding what is only his due. The French historian Michelet was incensed at the spectacle: "This poor man of genius, slaving away at interpreting and reporting the lucubrations of stupid men; indispensable intermediary between Soderini, the inept gonfalonier, and the equally inept Cardinal d'Amboise.... A considerable portion of his dispatches – and the whole of this particular one – is given over to complaints that he is starving to death and needs a new pair of trousers."

Magnificent Signori: –
I write these few lines for the purpose of recommending myself especially to your Lordships, knowing that I may do so with entire confidence. On leaving Florence I received thirty-three ducats, of which I have expended about thirteen for postage as per account sent to your colleague Niccolò d'Alessandro Machiavelli. Eighteen ducats I had to pay for a mule, and for a velvet suit eighteen more. For a Spanish cloak I paid eleven ducats, and for an overcoat ten, making in all seventy ducats. I am living at an hostelry which costs daily for myself and two servants and the mule ten carlini.

158

Charles VIII's triumphal entry into an Italian city

True, your Lordships have given me the salary I asked for;
and I asked for what I supposed would be sufficient, not
knowing how dear everything is here. I have therefore to
thank your Lordships, and to complain only of myself.
But having learned to know the cost of living here better,
I would now beg your Lordships to remedy the matter, if it
can be done. If my salary cannot be increased, at least have
me reimbursed for the postage expenses, as has always been
done to every envoy. Niccolò d'Allessandro Machiavelli
knows my circumstances, and can tell you whether I am
able to bear such a loss; and even if I could, your Lordships
know that in this age men labor to get ahead, and not to
go behindhand.

I recommend myself to your Lordships, *quae feliciter
valeant*.

NICCOLÒ MACHIAVELLI

Rome, 22 November, 1503.

Decisions

*As secretary to the Provveditori on their inspection trips
to the city fortifications, Machiavelli modestly claims that
he merely listened to what the architects and the military
officials had to say. But we know that he played a large
part in formulating the plans to rebuild the ramparts. Thanks
to his letters and contemporary engravings of Florence, we
have a clear picture of what these plans entailed. In what
follows, we see how Clement VII was interfering.*

To his Magnificence, Francesco Guicciardini
Magnificent President:
Since I have not spoken with you for several days about
the fortifications, I will now write you my views on the
subject. It is quite obvious hereabouts that the Pope has
gone back to his pet scheme for the hillside slopes [of San
Miniato], having been swayed by the opinion of Giovanni
del Bene, who wrote him that if the line of fortifications
were built so as to enclose the hillsides it would be stronger
and less expensive. As for being stronger, a city extending
over a large area is never very strong, for its great size
alone discourages its defenders and leaves the city open to a
thousand surprise attacks that cities of more modest size
have no reason to fear. As for its being less expensive, this

is mere humbug, and del Bene's opinion rests on a number of suppositions which are simply not true. In the first place, he says that we need only build escarpments on the slopes, from Bonciano's estates to Matteo Bartoli's – a distance he calculates to be a thousand yards, whereas it is really sixteen hundred – and that for the rest all we need is one wall. He says that the escarpments can take the place of walls and that all we need on top of them is a parapet four yards high and eight yards thick. This is an error: there are countless flat areas where escarpments cannot be cut away; as for those areas in which escarpments could be cut away, they would not hold; the soil would slip and a wall would be needed to shore it up. The parapets would cost a fortune; they would be a disgrace to our city; and in a few years they would have to be rebuilt; we would have to keep pouring enormous sums into this whole sorry project. He claims that the commune would acquire enclosed lands worth 80,000 ducats, but this is sheer nonsense; he doesn't know what he's saying and would be hard put to prove it. There is nobody who shares his opinion, yet the plan that the Pope requested will be drawn up and sent to him. (Familiar Letter 209, dated June 2, 1526.)

Warnings

Machiavelli even made a vain attempt to persuade his fellow citizens to take up arms against Cesare Borgia. In this speech he displays a brutal frankness quite different from the tone he employed when acting as "Their Magnificences' interpreter."

When I consider that you can see and hear, yet refuse to see or hear – to the point that even your enemies are, if nothing else, amazed – I am led to believe that God has not yet sufficiently punished us, and that he has still greater trials in store for us. . . . Do not tell me: "We had no warning.". . . And if you answer: "Why should we need arms? We are under the protection of the King [of France] . . . Duke Valentine has no reason to attack us," I shall reply that nothing could be farther from the truth. . . . Let us not seek to hide the truth from ourselves. Let us take a close look at the situation here at home. You will be forced to conclude that your subjects are disloyal, as was proved by your bitter experience of a few months ago. This was to be expected: no subjects can or should be loyal to a prince unable to defend them or to govern them. Pistoia, Borgo, the Romagna know exactly how well you have governed them, how well you will govern them: all these places have become a nest and refuge for all sorts of marauders. All the places that have been attacked know exactly how well you were able to defend them; and as your subjects do not find you any stronger today than you were yesterday, you may be quite certain that neither their opinions nor their state of mind has changed. They are not your subjects; they are the subjects of the first invader who happens to pass their way.

Now go outside your own territory and take a look at your neighbors: you are caught between two or three cities which would far rather see you die than live themselves. Go farther, leave Tuscany, consider the whole of Italy: you will see that all of it revolves about the King of France, Venice, the Pope, and Valentine. Begin with the King: here the truth must be told, and I shall be the one to say it. Either he will find in Italy no obstacle other than you to fear, in which case there is nothing to be done, for all your forces, all your conniving, will not save you; or else he will encounter other obstacles, as in fact he has before, in which case there is either something to be done, or nothing to be done, depending on whether you are willing to act or not. Instead of remaining disarmed and thus giving some other powerful prince the idea of snapping you up and selling you out to the King, and the King the idea of writing you off as a loss, what you can do is to acquire enough military strength so that he will respect you as much as he does others in Italy. This would make others respect you, and keep people from conceiving the idea of bringing you under their yoke. . . .

This is what I, for my part, refuse to believe of you, for I see that you are free citizens of Florence and see that your future freedom is in your own hands. I should like to believe it will be as precious to you as it has always been to those men who were born free and seek to live in freedom. (Urgent Remarks on the Needs to Raise Funds.)

Urgent Advice

In this dispatch, the humble servant of the Republic does

his utmost to stiffen the resolution of his despairing superiors:

For what sort of an arrangement can you expect from an enemy, who, despite of having the Alps between you and himself, and with the number of troops which you have on foot, still asks one hundred florins of you within the space of three days, and one hundred and fifty thousand within ten days? When he gets to Florence the first thing he will ask of you will be all the movable property you possess. For without doubt (would it were not so!) the only inducement they have for advancing is the hope of pillaging your city. And there is no other way of escaping these evils but to undeceive the enemy as to your ability to resist him; and if this is to be done, then it is better to do it in the mountains than within our city walls, and to employ all the forces we have to keep him there. For if the enemy is detained in the mountains but a short time he will have to disband, as we learn from reliable quarters that if they do not succeed within the present month in taking some one of the large places, in which they will not succeed unless the places are abandoned, then they must of necessity succumb. And even if you should not succeed in defending yourselves on the other side or within the mountains, there will be nothing to prevent you from bringing the forces which you have over there to this side. For I remember in the war with Pisa, that the Pisans, wearied by its long duration, began to discuss amongst themselves whether they ought not to make terms with you. Pandolfo Petrucci, anticipating such an attempt, sent Messer Antonio da Venafro to dissuade them from it. Messer Antonio addressed them in public meeting, and after many other things said to them, "that they had passed a very tempestuous sea, and wanted now to drown themselves in a well." I do not mention this because I think that Florence is about to abandon herself to despair, but to give you certain hope of safety provided you are willing rather to spend ten florins to secure your safety, than forty that would serve to enslave and ruin you. I recommend myself to your Lordships, *quae bene valeant.*

Servitor

NICCOLÒ MACHIAVELLI

Bologna, 2 April, 1527.

(Official Letter 16 to the Eight.)

"THE FRUITS OF HISTORY"

The Ex-Diplomat

For nearly a year, Machiavelli had fondly hoped that his friend Vettori, Florence's representative at the papal court, in Rome, could somehow find him a post there. As he phrased it, even "rolling rocks" would do. But now he writes Vettori to forget about it.

So I shall stay on here among these lice of mine, without finding anybody who remembers my record in service or who thinks I am good for anything. But I can't continue very long in this way. My funds are giving out and I can see that if the Almighty does not show Himself better disposed towards me, I shall some day be obliged to leave home, take a post as reader or bookkeeper to some constable, if I can't do any better, or go to some out of the way place to teach children their letters, allowing the people here, meantime, to imagine that I am dead. For that matter I am quite a burden to them. I am in the habit of spending, and cannot do without spending. I am not saying all this with the idea that you are to put yourself to any trouble or inconvenience in my behalf, but just to get this wretched matter off my chest and never mention it to you again. . . . (Letter to Vettori, dated June 10, 1514.)

Retirement at San Casciano

This is the most revealing of Machiavelli's letters. The reader can judge for himself just how well Niccolò understood himself when he defined his own highest value (solum mio) as the very opposite of Leonardo da Vinci's. The letter is also valuable for the light it throws on the origin and purpose of The Prince. *And it comes as rather a surprise to discover that Alfred de Musset's* Les Voeux stériles *(Vain Hopes, 1821) contains an admirable translation of the most moving passage in this letter, the few brief lines in which Machiavelli rails at Fate.*

I am living on my farm, and since my last troubles I have not been in Florence twenty days, putting them all together. Up to now I have been setting snares for thrushes with my own hands; I get up before daylight, prepare my birdlime, and go out with a bundle of cages on my back, so that I look like Geta when he came back from the harbor with the books of Amphitryo, and catch at the least two thrushes and at the most six. So I did all of September; then this trifling diversion, despicable and strange as it is, to my regret failed. What my life is now I shall tell you.

In the morning I get up with the sun and go out into a grove that I am having cut; there I remain a couple of hours to look over the work of the past day and kill some time with the woodmen, who always have on hand some dispute either among themselves or among their neighbors. And as to this grove I could tell you a thousand good things that have happened in my dealings with Frosino da Panzano and others who wanted some firewood from it. Frosino in particular sent for several cords of wood without saying anything to me about them, and when he paid for them he wished to keep back ten lire, which he said he won from me four years ago when he beat me at *cricca* in the house of Antonio Guicciardini. I began to raise the devil, and was intending to accuse the drayman who had come for the wood of theft, but Giovanni Machiavelli stepped in between us and got us to agree. Batista Guicciardini, Filippo Ginori, Tommaso del Bene and certain other citizens each agreed to take a cord of wood when the north wind was blowing. I promised all of them and sent a cord to Tommaso, which turned out half a cord at Florence, because his wife, the servants, and his children were all there to pile it up; they looked like Gabburra when on Thursday he and his servants club an ox. Hence, having seen who was getting the profit, I told the others I had no more wood, and all of them have got angry about it, and especially Batista, who puts this in the same class as his losses at the sack of Prato.

When I leave the grove, I go to a spring, and from there into my aviary. I have a book in my pocket, either Dante or Petrarch or one of the minor poets, as Tibullus, Ovid, and the like. I read about their tender passions and their loves, remember mine, and take pleasure for a while in thinking about them. Then I go along the road to the inn, talk with those who pass by, ask the news of their villages, learn various things and note the varied tastes and different fancies of men. It gets to be dinner time, and with my troop I eat what food my poor farm and my little property permit. After dinner, I return to the inn; there I usually find the host, a butcher, a miller, and two furnace-tenders. With these fellows I sink into vulgarity for the rest of the day, playing at *cricca* and *trich-trach;* from these games come a thousand quarrels and numberless offensive and insulting words; we often dispute over a penny, and all the same are heard shouting as far as San Casciano. So, involved in these trifles, I keep my brain from getting mouldy, and express the perversity of Fate, for I am willing to have her drive me along this path, to see if she will be ashamed of it.

In the evening, I return to my house, and go into my study. At the door I take off the clothes I have worn all day, mud spotted and dirty, and put on regal and courtly garments. Thus appropriately clothed, I enter into the ancient courts of ancient men, where, being lovingly received, I feed on the food which alone is mine, and which I was born for; I am not ashamed to speak with them and to ask the reasons for their actions, and they courteously answer me. For four hours I feel no boredom and forget every worry; I do not fear poverty, and death does not terrify me. I give myself completely over to the ancients. And because Dante says that there is no knowledge unless one retains what one has read, I have written down the profit I have gained from their conversation, and composed a little book *De principatibus,* in which I go as deep as I can into reflections on this subject, debating what a principate is, what the species are, how they are gained, how they are kept, and why they are lost. If ever any of my trifles can please you, this one should not displease you; and to a prince, and especially a new prince, it ought to be welcome. Hence I am dedicating it to His Magnificence Giuliano. Filippo Casavecchia has seen it; he will be able to tell you something about the thing in itself and the talks I have had with him, though I am all the time enlarging and repolishing it.

You wish, Honorable Ambassador, that I give up my present life and come to enjoy yours with you. I shall do so in any case, but what tempts me now is a certain affair of mine that I can finish inside of six weeks. What makes me hesitate is that the Soderini are there, and if I went to Rome I should be obliged to visit them and talk with them. I fear that at my return I could not hope to dismount at home, but should dismount at the Bargello, because, even though this government has very strong foundations and great security, yet it is new, and therefore suspicious, and there are plenty of wiseacres who, to appear like Pagolo Bertini, would seat others at the dinner table and let me think about paying the bill. I pray you to settle this doubt for me, and then I surely shall come to visit you within the time I have set.

I have debated with Filippo about this little work of mine, whether it was wise to give it or not to give it [to Giuliano]; and if it were wise to give it whether it would be wise to carry it myself or to send it to you. If I do not give it, I fear that, to say the least, it will not be read by Giuliano, and that this Ardinghelli would get honor from this last labor of mine. The pressure of necessity inclines me to give it, because I am wearing myself out, and cannot remain long in my present state without getting so poor that I shall be despised. Then there is my hope that these Medici lords will begin to employ me, even if they begin by making me roll a stone, because if I did not then gain them over to me, I would have only myself to blame. This thing I have written, if it came to be read, would show that I have not been asleep or playing for the fifteen years that I have devoted to the study of the art of the state. Anybody should be glad to get the services of one who has had a great deal of experience at the expense of others. They should not hesitate over my faith, because, since I have always kept my faith,

I am not likely to learn how to break it now. He who has been faithful and good for forty-three years, as I have, is hardly able to change his nature, and my poverty is a testimony to both my faith and my goodness.

I hope, then, that you will write to me your opinion on this matter, and I present my respects. I wish you success.

NICCOLÒ MACHIAVELLI in Florence

December 10, 1513.

(*Familiar Letter 148* to Vettori.)

Machiavelli would have agreed with Stendhal's statement that he "had always loathed silly exhibitions of family feeling." What Machiavelli said on this score was, "It has always been hard for me to speak of myself and of those close to me." This remark should be checked against the sonnet he wrote to Messer Bernardo, his father, against the touching Familiar Letters 222 and 226, and against the following scrawled letters in his wife's handwritting. From them, the reader may decide for himself whether Machiavelli ever shared the blessings of Dante's Ulysses: "his son's devotion, his aged father's piety, and Penelope's ever-faithful love."

MARIETTA CORSINI TO NICCOLÒ MACHIAVELLI

My very dear Niccolò,

You make fun of me, but you are not right. I should be more courageous, if you were here. You well know that I am never in good spirits when you are away, and less than ever now that I hear that there is the plague in Rome. Imagine if I can be happy, when I can rest neither by night nor day. Please, write more frequently than you do now; I have received only three letters from you. Do not be surprised, if I have not written you; it was impossible; I was sick in bed with fever. The baby is well and resembles you. He is white as snow, but his head is like a bit of black velvet, and he is hairy as you are. His resemblance to you makes me think him beautiful, and he is as lively as though he were a year old, and he opened his eyes before he was quite born, and made his voice heard all over the house. But the little girl is not at all well. Do come back. Nothing else. God be with you and bless you.

I am sending your night cap, two shirts, two handkerchiefs, and a towel. Yours, Marietta, in Florence.

To Save the Nation

Machiavelli was very fond of his own children. However, as his panegyrics of Caterina Sforza and – see below – of Brutus in ancient Rome indicate, he believed that in exceptional circumstances the maintenance of freedom might require the sacrifice both of legal rights and ties of blood.

WHEN LIBERTY HAS BEEN NEWLY ACQUIRED IT IS NECESSARY IN ORDER TO MAINTAIN IT TO "KILL THE SONS OF BRUTUS"

The severity used by Brutus was no less necessary than it was useful in maintaining the liberty which Rome had just acquired by his aid. Of such severity one rarely comes across a case in history in which a father not only sits on a tribunal and condemns his own sons to death, but is present at their death. Those, however, who are familiar with ancient history are well aware that, when the form of government has been changed, whether from a republic to a tyranny or a tyranny to a republic, it is in all cases essential that exemplary action be taken against those who are hostile to the new state of affairs. He who establishes a tyranny and does not kill 'Brutus,' and he who establishes a democratic regime and does not kill 'the Sons of Brutus, will not last long.

Since this question has already been discussed at length elsewhere I refer the reader back to what was there said, and shall here give but one example, a modern one, which took place in our own day in our own country. It is that of Peter Soderini who thought that by patience and goodness he could quell the desire of "Brutus's sons" to return to another form of government, but in this he was mistaken. Though, being a prudent man, he should have recognized the need for action, and though the type of ambitious men who were against him gave him ground for getting rid of them, yet he could never make up his mind to do this. For, in addition to thinking that he could by patience and goodness extinguish their malevolence, and by distributing rewards put an end to some of their hostility, he was of opinion – and often told his friends so in confidence – that, if he were to take vigorous action against his opponents and to fight his adversaries, he would need to assume extraordinary authority and introduce laws disruptive of civic equality; and that such a course and such authority, even though he did not henceforth use it tyrannically, would so alarm the general public that, after his death, they would never again agree to appoint a gonfalonier for life, an office which he thought it would be well to strengthen and to keep up.

Such a point of view was wise and good. None the less, an evil should never be allowed to continue out of respect for a good when that good may easily be overwhelmed by that evil. Soderini ought to have considered that, when his actions and his intentions came to be judged by their end and in the light of the good fortune and the life that had accompanied them, he would be able to convince everyone that what he had done, was done for the security of his country, and not for ambitious reasons. He could, more-over, so have regulated things that none of his successors could do with evil intent what he had done with good intent. But the view which he first adopted misled him, for he failed to realize that malevolence is not vanquished by time, nor placated by any gifts. With the result that, through his inability to emulate Brutus, he lost both his position and his reputation, a loss in which his country shared. (Discourses III, III.)

We saw above how Caterina Sforza, who had already made up her mind, attempted to pull the wool over Niccolò's eyes by feigning indecision. That lesson in womanly wiles occurred at Forli in 1499. Now, much later he cites her as an outstanding example of manly magnanimity:

Some conspirators who were citizens of Forli, killed Count Girolamo, their Lord, and took prisoners his wife and his children, who were little ones. It seemed to them, however, that their lives would scarce be safe unless they could get hold of the citadel, which its governor declined to hand over. So Mistress Catherine, as the countess was called, promised the conspirators that, if they would let her go to the citadel, she would arrange for it to be handed over to them. Meanwhile they were to keep her children as hostages. On this understanding the conspirators let her o to the citadel, from the walls of which, when she got inside, she reproached them with killing her husband and threatened them with vengeance in every shape and form.

171

And to convince them that she did not mind about her children she exposed herself and said she was still capable of bearing more. The conspirators, dumbfounded, realized their mistake too late, and paid the penalty for their lack of prudence by suffering perpetual banishment. (*Discourses, III*, vi.)

As to the second piece of advice in relation to fortresses, I say, that nothing can expose a fortress to greater danger, than to have places of retreat into which the garrison may retire when they are hard pressed; for if it was not for the hopes of finding safety in one post, after they have abandoned another, they would exert themselves with more obstinacy and resolution in defending the first; and when that is deserted, all the rest will soon fall into the enemy's hand. Of this we have a recent and memorable instance in the loss of the citadel at Forli, when the countess Catharine was besieged there by Cesare Borgia, son to Pope Alexander VI at the head of a French army. That fortress was so full of such places of retreat, that a garrison might retire out of one into another, and out of that into many more successively upon occasion. For in the first place there was the citadel; and in the next, a castle, separated from it by a ditch, with a draw-bridge upon it, over which you might go out of one into the other; and in this castle there were three divisions, separated from one another by ditches full of water, with draw-bridges over them. The duke, therefore, having made a breach in the wall of one of these divisions with his artillery, Giovanni da Casale, who was the governor, instead of defending the breach, retreated into another division; upon which the duke's forces immediately entered that division without opposition, and having got possession of the draw-bridges, soon made themselves masters of all the rest. The loss of that fortress, then, which was thought inexpugnable, was owing to two great errors; the first in making so many conveniences of retreating from one place to another, and the second, in that none of those places could command their bridges; so that the ill contrivance of the fortress, and the want of conduct in the garrison, defeated the magnanimous resolution of the countess, who had the courage to wait for an army there, which neither the king of Naples nor the duke of Milan durst face: however, though her efforts did not succeed, she gained much

Marco Palmezzano: Caterina Sforza

reputation by so generous a stand, as appears from many copies of verses made in her praise upon that occasion. (*The Art of War,* VII.)

Indecisive Republics

Just before war broke out between Louis XII of France and Ludovico il Moro, with the result (stipulated by the treaty of Blois) that Lombardy was sliced up between France and Venice, Machiavelli reflected on the irresolute state of mind of his native Florence.

Meanwhile the undercover campaign of the French against Milan was being stepped up.... The Duke of Milan, being only too well aware of the dangers threatening him, made overtures to us and strongly urged us to join him.... He asked us for three hundred men-at-arms and two thousand infantrymen. Our course in such circumstances was fraught with difficulties: it was dangerous to stall for time with Milan and France, and the latter was applying great pressure to get us to come out openly against the Duke, and requested five hundred men-at-arms and three thousand foot-soldiers. We sent both of them the reply that

173

we could not take sides openly so long as matters in Pisa were not settled, and promised each of them that we would join his side as soon as we had recovered this city. This hesitation resulted in our serving neither God nor the Devil; and the French in particular greatly resented this. (*Notes for the History of Florence*, IX.)

The Ancients as Models

Much in the tone of some old military captain who feels he has been born too late, in an era of wars much less noble than his training has prepared him for, here Machiavelli the statesman, the sharp-eyed civil servant, bewails his fate: he has never found the sort of masters he has always dreamed of serving. As in the History of Florence, Machiavelli here "lets himself go" (mi sfogo).

Before our Italian princes had been scourged by the Ultramontanes, they thought it sufficient for a prince to write a handsome letter, or return a civil answer to one; to excel in drollery and repartee; to undermine and deceive one another; and to set themselves off with jewels and lace; to eat and sleep in greater magnificence and luxury than their neighbours; to spend their time in wanton dalliance and lascivious pleasures; to keep up a haughty kind of state, and grind the faces of their subjects; to indulge themselves in indolence and inactivity; to dispose of their military honours and preferments to pimps and parasites; to neglect and despise merit of every kind, to browbeat those that endeavoured to point out any thing that was salutary or praise-worthy; to have their words and sayings looked upon as oracles; not foreseeing, (weak and infatuated as they were) that by such conduct they were making a rod for their own backs, and exposing themselves to the mercy of the first invader. To this were owing the dreadful alarms, the disgraceful defeats, and the astonishing losses they sustained in the year one thousand four hundred and ninety five; and hence it came to pass three of the most powerful states in Italy were so often ravaged and laid waste in those times. But it is still more deplorable to see that those princes, who are yet left in possession of any domains, are so far from taking warning from the downfall of others, that they pursue the same course, and live in the same sort of misrule and fatal security; not considering that princes in former times, who were desirous either to acquire new dominion, or at least to preserve their own, strictly observed all those rules which I have laid down and recommended in the course of this conversation, and that their chief endeavours were to inure their bodies to all manner of hardship and fatigue, and to fortify their minds against danger and the fear of death. Thus Julius Caesar, Alexander of Macedon, and many other great men and heroic princes, whom I have mentioned before, always fought at the head of their own armies, always marched with them on foot, and carried their own arms; and if any of them ever lost their power, they lost their life with it at the same time, and died with the same reputation and glory which they had always maintained whilst they lived. . . .

. . . and for my own part, I cannot help complaining of Fortune, which should either not have suffered me to know these things, or give me power to put them into execution; which is a thing I cannot hope for, now I am so far advanced in years. For which reason, I have freely communicated my thoughts to you of this matter, as young men and well qualified not only to instil such advice into the ears of your princes, if you approve of it, but to assist them in carrying it into execution whenever a proper opportunity shall offer; and let me conjure you not to despair of success, since this province seems destined to revive arts and sciences which have seemed long since dead; as we see it has already raised poetry, painting, and sculpture, as it were, from the grave. As to myself, indeed, I cannot expect to see so happy a change at my time of life; but if Fortune had indulged me some years ago with a territory fit for such an undertaking, I think I soon should have convinced the world of the excellency of the ancient military discipline; for I would either have increased my own dominions with glory, or at least not have lost them with infamy and disgrace. (*Art of War, VII*, XVII.)

On the Evils of Mercenaries

After reviewing examples from the history of Rome, Sparta, Carthage, and Thebes, and then the more recent examples of the Swiss and the Milanese enslaved by Francesco Sforza, Machiavelli brings the record up to date:

The Florentines appointed Paolo Vitelli their captain, a man of great prudence, who had risen from a private station to the highest reputation. If he had taken Pisa no one can deny that it was highly important for the Florentines to retain his friendship, because had he become the soldier of their enemies they would have had no means of opposing him; and if they had retained him they would have been obliged to obey him. As to the Venetians, if one considers the progress they made, it will be seen that they acted surely and gloriously so long as they made war with their own forces; that it was before they commenced their enterprises on land that they fought courageously with their own gentlemen and armed populace, but when they began to fight on land they abandoned this virtue, and began to follow the Italian custom. And at the commencement of their land conquests they had not much to fear from their captains, their territories not being very large, and their reputation being great, but as their possessions increased, as they did under Carmagnola, they had an example of their mistake. For seeing that he was very powerful, after he had defeated the Duke of Milan, and knowing, on the other hand, that he was but lukewarm in this war, they considered that they would not make any more conquests with him, and they neither would nor could dismiss him, for fear of losing what they had already gained. In order to make sure of him they were therefore obliged to execute him . . . for with these forces, only slow and trifling acquisitions are made, but sudden and miraculous losses . . . the result of their prowess has been that Italy has been overrun by Charles, preyed on by Louis, tyrannised over by Ferrando, and insulted by the Swiss. (*The Prince,* Chapter XII.)

"The Romans gave to Army Commanders Discretionary Powers"

Although Machiavelli never expressly formulated a conception of the "separation of powers," as such, he was well on the way to it. Distinguishing between the executive political power and that of the Army, he condemns the serious confusion of the Signori on this score and therein sees one of the reasons why the war with Pisa lasted twelve long years.

If one is to profit from the perusal of Livy's history one ought, I think, to take account of all the modes of procedure used by the people and senate of Rome and amongst other points worthy of notice there is the authority we find them giving to their consul, dictators, and other army commanders when in the field. It was of a very high order, for the senate reserved to itself only the power to initiate fresh wars and to confirm peace treaties. All else was left to the discretion and power of the consul. For, when the people and senate had decided to go to war, against the Latins, for instance, they left everything else to the discretion of the consul, who could either give battle or not give it, and attack this or that town as he thought fit.

This is confirmed by numerous examples, but especially by what occurred in an expedition against the Tuscans. The consul, Fabius, had defeated those who were near Sutrium, and was planning next to lead his army through the Ciminian forest en route for Tuscany. About this, not only did he not consult the senate, but he did not even inform them, though the war was to be carried on in a new, unexplored, and dangerous country. Further confirmation is afforded by the action the senate here took, which was of the opposite kind; for, when they heard of the victory which Fabius had gained and wondered whether his next step would be to pass through the said forest into Tuscany, they thought it best not to run the risk this war would entail, and so sent two legates to Fabius to stop him from going on to Tuscany. But, when they arrived, he had already got there and had won a victory, so that, instead of preventing a war, the legates came home bringing news of a conquest and of glory won. . . .

. . . To this I have the more willingly called attention, because I notice that the republics of today, such as the Venetian and the Florentine republics, act differently, for if their generals, administrators or commissioners, have to set up a piece of artillery, they want to know of it and to advise about it – a procedure as praiseworthy as are others of that ilk, which together have brought us to our present pass. (*Discourses, II,* XXXIII.)

The Eternal Recurrence of the Forms of Government

Machiavelli found peace of mind in reflecting on a certain stability in the working out of political forms, in this respect resembling Leonardo da Vinci.

For in the beginning of the world, when its inhabitants were few, they lived for a time scattered like the beasts. Then, with the multiplication of their offspring, they drew together and, in order the better to be able to defend themselves, began to look about for a man stronger and more courageous than the rest, made him their head, and obeyed him.

It was thus that men learned how to distinguish what is honest and good from what is pernicious and wicked, for the sight of someone injuring his benefactor evoked in them hatred and sympathy and they blamed the ungrateful and respected those who showed gratitude, well aware that the same injuries might have been done to themselves. Hence to prevent evil of this kind they took to making laws and to assigning punishments to those who contravened them. The notion of justice thus came into being.

In this way it came about that, when later on they had to choose a prince, they did not have recourse to the boldest as formerly, but to one who excelled in prudence and justice.

But when at a yet later stage they began to make the prince hereditary instead of electing him, his heirs soon began to degenerate as compared with their ancestors, and, forsaking virtuous deeds, considered that princes had naught else to do but to surpass other men in extravagance, lasciviousness, and every other form of licentiousness. With the result that the prince came to be hated, and, since he was hated, came to be afraid, and from fear soon passed to offensive action which quickly brought about a tyranny.

From which, before long, was begotten the source of their downfall; for tyranny gave rise to conspiracies and plots against princes, organized not by timid and weak men, but by men conspicuous for their liberality, magnanimity, wealth and ability, for such men could not stand the dishonorable life the prince was leading. The masses, therefore, at the instigation of these powerful leaders, took up arms against the prince, and, when he had been liquidated, submitted to the authority of those whom they looked upon as their liberators. Hence the latter, to whom the very term 'sole head' had become odious, formed themselves into a government. Moreover, in the beginning, mindful of what they had suffered under a tyranny, they ruled in accordance with the laws which they had made, subordinated their own convenience to the common advantage, and, both in private matters and public affairs, governed and preserved order with the utmost diligence.

But when the administration passed to their descendants who had no experience of the changeability of fortune, had not been through bad times, and instead of remaining content with the civic equality then prevailing, reverted to avarice, ambition, and to seizing other men's womenfolk, they caused government by an aristocracy to become government by an oligarchy in which civic rights were entirely disregarded; so that in a short time there came to pass in their case the same thing as happened to the tyrant, for the masses, sick of their government, were ready to help anyone who had any sort of plan for attacking their rulers; and so there soon arose someone who with the aid of the masses liquidated them.

Then, since the memory of the prince and of the injuries inflicted by him was still fresh, and since, having got rid of government by the few, they had no desire to return to that of a prince, they turned to a democratic form of government, which they organized in such a way that no sort of authority was vested either in a few powerful men or in a prince.

And, since all forms of government are to some extent respected at the outset, this democratic form of government maintained itself for a while but not for long, especially when the generation that had organized it had passed away. For anarchy quickly supervened, in which no respect was shown either for the individual or for the official, and which was such that, as everyone did what he liked, all sorts of outrages were constantly committed. The outcome was inevitable. Either at the suggestion of some good man or because this anarchy had to be got rid of somehow, principality was once again restored. . . . This, then, is the cycle through which all commonwealths pass, whether they govern themselves or are governed. (*The Discourses, I,* ii.)

THE TECHNIQUE OF POWER

I

All states and dominions which hold or have held sway over mankind are either republics or monarchies. Monarchies are either hereditary in which the rulers have been for many years of the same family, or else they are of recent foundation. The newly founded ones are either entirely new, as was Milan to Francesco Sforza, or else they are, as it were, new members grafted on to the hereditary possessions of the prince that annexes them, as is the kingdom of Naples to the King of Spain. The dominions thus acquired have either been previously accustomed to the rule of another prince, or else have been free states, and they are annexed either by force of arms of the prince himself, or of others, or else fall to him by good fortune or special ability. (*The Prince*, Chapter I.)

II

I will not here speak of republics, having already treated of them fully in another place. I will deal only with monarchies, and will discuss how the various kinds described above

181

Portrait of Savonarola (San Pietro Martire)

can be governed and maintained. In the first place, the difficulty of maintaining hereditary states accustomed to a reigning family is far less than in new monarchies; for it is sufficient not to transgress ancestral usages, and to adapt one's self to unforeseen circumstances; in this way such a prince, if of ordinary assiduity, will always be able to maintain his position, unless some very exceptional and excessive force deprives him of it. . . . (*The Prince*, Chapter II.)

In What Way Princes Must Keep Faith

How laudable it is for a prince to keep good faith and live with integrity, and not with astuteness, every one knows. Still the experience of our times shows those princes to have done great things who have had little regard for good faith, and have been able by astuteness to confuse men's brains, and who have ultimately overcome those who have made loyalty their foundation.

You must know, then, that there are two methods of fighting, the one by law, the other by force: the first method is that of men, the second of beasts; but as the first method is often insufficient, one must have recourse to the second. It is therefore necessary for a prince to know well how to use both the beast and the man. This was covertly taught to rulers by ancient writers, who relate how Achilles and many others of those ancient princes were given to Chiron the centaur to be brought up and educated under his discipline. The parable of this semi-animal, semi-human teacher is meant to indicate that a prince must know how to use both natures, and that the one without the other is not durable.

A prince being thus obliged to know well how to act as a beast must imitate the fox and the lion, for the lion cannot protect himself from traps, and the fox cannot defend himself from wolves. One must therefore be a fox to recognise traps, and a lion to frighten wolves. Those that wish to be only lions do not understand this. Therefore, a prudent ruler ought not to keep faith when by so doing it would be against his interest, and when the reasons which made him bind himself no longer exist. If men were all good, this precept would not be a good one; but as they are bad, and would not observe their faith with you, so you are not bound to keep faith with them. Nor have legitimate grounds ever failed a prince who wished to show colourable excuse for the non-fulfilment of his promise. Of this one could furnish an infinite number of modern examples, and show how many times peace has been broken, and how many promises rendered worthless, by the faithlessness of princes, and those that have been best able to imitate the fox have succeeded best. But it is necessary to be able to disguise this character well, and to be a great feigner and dissembler; and men are so simple and so ready to obey present necessities, that one who deceives will always find those who allow themselves to be deceived. . . .

It is not, therefore, necessary for a prince to have all the above-named qualities, but it is very necessary to seem to have them. I would even be bold to say that to possess them and always to observe them is dangerous, but to appear to possess them is useful. Thus it is well to seem merciful, faithful, humane, sincere, religious, and also to be so; but you must have the mind so disposed that when it is needful to be otherwise you may be able to change to the opposite qualities. And it must be understood that a prince, and especially a new prince, cannot observe all those things which are considered good in men, being often obliged, in order to maintain the state, to act against faith, against charity, against humanity, and against religion. And, therefore, he must have a mind disposed to adapt itself according to the wind, and as the variations of fortune dictate, and, as I said before, not deviate from what is good, if possible, but the able to do evil if constrained. (*The Prince*, Chapter XVIII.)

In the first set of his Discourses, *or commentaries on the first ten books of Livy, written in 1506, Machiavelli made some undignified gibes at "the unarmed prophet," whose "divine radiance" had been dimmed "in a stronger fire." Sixteen years later, he found two occasions for going back to the topic of Savonarola, and although he now moderated his language, his attitude remained as irreverent as before. Contrasting Savonarola with Appius, tenth king of Rome, who was much later to provide Alfieri with the hero of his best tragedy* (Virginia), *Machiavelli went on to formulate one of his prime maxims of government:*

For I do not think a worse example can be set in a republic than to make a law and not to observe it; and when it is not observed by the man who made it so much the worse.

After '94 the government of Florence was reconstituted with the aid of Friar Girolamo Savonarola, whose writings attest the learning, prudence, and virtue of his mind. For the security of the citizens he had made, amongst other constitutions, a law which allowed an appeal to the people from a judgment which, in cases of treason, the Eight and the Signoria had passed. He had advocated this law for some time, and with the greatest difficulty got it accepted. Shortly after it had been sanctioned, it happened that five citizens were condemned to death by the Signoria for treason. When they wished to appeal they were not allowed to do so, and the law was not observed. This did more to lessen the reputation of the Friar than anything else that befell him. For, if the right to appeal was worth having, he ought to have seen that it was observed. If it was not worth having, he should not have forced it through. The event attracted more notice in that this Friar in no one of the many sermons which he preached after the law had been broken, ever condemned the breach or offered any excuse. For, since it suited his purpose, to condemn it he was unwilling, and to excuse it he was unable. Since this made it plain to all that at heart he was ambitious and a party-man, it ruined his reputation and brought on him much reproach. (*Discourses, I,* xlv.)

What Machiavelli condemned as rashness and madness seven years before, he is now led by his study of the past to recognize as a factor in political success.

RESULTS ARE OFTEN OBTAINED BY IMPETUOSITY AND DARING
WHICH COULD NEVER HAVE BEEN OBTAINED
BY ORDINARY METHODS

... if one ruler desires to get something from another, he should, when circumstances permit, not give him time for consideration, but should act in such a way that he will see the need of a prompt decision, which he will do if he sees that to refuse what is asked or to postpone the matter will at once arouse resentment that may be dangerous.

We find that such means have been effectively employed in our own times by Pope Julius in his dealings with the French, and by Monsieur de Foix, the French king's general, in dealing with the Marquess of Mantua. For when Pope Julius wanted to expel the Bentivogli from Bologna, he realized that he would require French forces for this, and that the Venetians must remain neutral. So he approached them both, but, on receiving ambiguous and discrepant answers, he decided to bring both of them around to his point of view by giving them no time to do aught else. So he set out from Rome with such forces as he could muster, and approached Bologna, sending at the same time messages telling the Venetians to remain neutral and the King of France to send troops. Whereupon, since there was left to them but a brief space of time, and since the Pope would obviously become highly indignant if they hesitated or refused, they yielded to his wishes, and the king sent help and the Venetians remained neutral.

Similarly, when Monsieur de Foix, then at Bologna with his army, heard that Brescia had rebelled and wanted to go and recover it, he had two ways to go: one through territory belonging to the king, a long and tedious route; the other a short route through Mantuan territory. The latter route would not only mean that he had to pass through the dominion of the Marquess, but that he would also have to enter it by certain routes which lay between marshes and lakes wherein that region abounds, and which were locked and guarded by the Marquess with castles and other defenses. Wherefore, de Foix, having decided to go by the short route, to obviate any difficulty he did not give the Marquess time to consider, but at once marched with his troops along this road, and notified the Marquess that he should hand him the keys to pass through. Whereupon the Marquess, bewildered by this sudden decision, sent him the keys. This he would never have done if de Foix had been more hesitant in his behavior. . . . (*Discourses, III,* xliv.)

The art of keeping satellites in line involves such measures as occupation, deportation, or extermination. Here are his recommendations regarding Arezzo, a city that was little more than a satellite of Florence:

Last year Arezzo, and all the territory in the Val di Chiana, followed the example of the Latin peoples fairly closely: first there was rebellion, followed by repression. . . . there were, however, certain differences. If it is true that history teaches us how to act, it would have been a good thing, when faced with the task of meting out justice and punishing the populace of the Val di Chiana, to follow the example of those who made themselves the masters of the world, especially when they teach so clear a lesson in the art of governing: they knew how to make the punishment fit the crime. So should you, since you too are faced with many different sorts of crimes on the part of those who rebel against you.

If you say: "But that is just what we have done!" I shall reply: "In particular cases, perhaps, but not in principle." I believe that you have done well in letting the people of Cortona, Castiglione, il Borgo, and Foiano retain all their local associations, in flattering them, in winning them over by granting them favors, for I think their case is not unlike that of the Lanuvini, the Aricini, the Nomentani, the Tusculani, and the Pedani, whom the Romans treated in much the same way. But I do not approve of the way you dealt with the Aretini, who deserve as little consideration as the Veliterni and the Anziani [in the days of the Romans]; yet they were treated quite differently. Just as the procedure of the Romans merits praise, so yours deserves blame. The Romans thought it necessary either to win rebellious peoples over to their side, or to annihilate them, considering any other solution to be fraught with perils. To my mind, you have followed no such course with the Aretini: I do not call it granting favors to have summoned them to Florence day after day, to have stripped them of all their honor, to have auctioned off their property, to have publicly vilified them, to have kept occupation troops in their territory; I do not consider that you have protected yourself against Arezzo if you leave its ramparts still standing and five-sixths of its inhabitants still living there, without forcing them to take in immigrants, so that in the event of hostilities or wars it would not cost you more money to keep the Aretini in bondage than you would spend to fight off your aggressors from without. (*Remarks on the Urgent Need to Raise Funds.*)

LAST WORDS

LETTER TO VETTORI

Monsignor della Motta went to the camp of the Imperials today with the text of the agreement that had been established in Rome. If Bourbon wants to accept the agreement he will halt his army. If he advances, it will be a sign of his refusal. In other words, tomorrow will decide what our lot will be. Here, in Florence, we have decided that if he advances, we will think of war and nothing else, giving not one shred of attention to talk of peace. If he halts, we will consider peace and lay aside every thought of war. With this wind that is blowing, you too must mind the tiller. If the decision is war, you must break off all dickering with peace, so that the Allies will dash forward, head down. Here there must be no limping and hopping. We must rush madly in, for despair often finds devices that cold choice has failed to find. The Imperials are advancing without artillery and over rough ground. If, therefore, we can combine the little life we have left with the forces of the League, which are in good shape, the Imperials will either retire from that territory in confusion or else come to a more reasonable frame of mind. I love Francesco Guicciardini, but I love my

187

country more than my very soul. I can tell you this, with sixty years of experience behind me: we have never been in a more ticklish situation than this one, where peace is necessary but war cannot be avoided, and where we are called upon to deal with a prince who, doing his utmost, can contribute either to peace alone or to war alone. I commend myself to you. Addi 16 d'Aprile 1527.

GUIDO MACHIAVELLI TO NICCOLÒ MACHIAVELLI

To His Honorable Father Niccolò Machiavelli

Forli

Jhesus

Honorable Father I greet you, etc. This is in answer to your letter of April 2nd from which we learn that you are well; God be praised and keep you well.

You were not informed about Totto, because he is not yet at home, but the husband of the wet nurse told us that his eyes are not yet recovered; he says, however, that he is improving; so you must be of good cheer. The small mule has not been sent to Monte Pugliano, because the grass has not come up yet; as soon as the weather is settled, it will be sent anyway.

From the letter you wrote to Monna Marietta we heard of the very beautiful chain you bought for Baccina; she is thinking all the time of this nice little chain, and she prays God for you, that you may come back soon.

We do not think any more about the lansquenets, because you promised us that you would try to join us, if anything happens; hereafter, Monna Marietta has no more to fear.

We beg you to let us know when the enemies intend to come against us, because we have still many things in the farm, wine and oil, although we have already brought here twenty or twenty-three barrels of oil, and we keep them here. According to your letter, we asked Sagrino if he were willing to keep in his house the things to which you referred, and he agreed. Please inform us about the enemies because it will take two or three days to accomplish these small things in San Casciano. We are all in good health, and I feel perfectly well, and I will begin at Easter, when Baccio is recovered, to study my music, playing, singing and studying counterpoint. If we both are well, I hope within a month to be able to play without him, God helping. As to the grammar, I begin today the participles: Mr. Luca has taught me almost all the first book of the Metamorphoseos [sic] of Ovid; and I propose when you are back, to tell you all the poem by heart.

Monna Marietta wishes to remain in your good graces; she sends you two shirts, two towels, two night caps, three pairs of stockings and four handkerchiefs. She also asks you to come back soon, and we all join her in this. Christ protect you and keep you in good health. From Florence, April 17th, MDXXVII.

Yours Guido Machiavelli in Florence

MACHIAVELLI TO HIS SON GUIDO

To Guido, son of Niccolò Machiavelli

Imola, April 2, 1527.

I have received your letter and it was a great joy to me, especially because it told me that you are well again. No news could have made me happier. If the Lord vouchsafes life to you, and to me as well, I believe I can make something of you, especially if you do all that you ought. In addition to the important people who have been friends with me all along, I have now made friends with Cardinal Cibo – so great a friendship, indeed, that I am quite astonished. This connection will stand you in good stead. But you have got to educate yourself. Since you have no further excuse for doing wrong, work hard, learn your literature and your music. You see all the consideration that comes to me from the little talent that I have. So, my boy, if you would make me happy, be successful and a credit to yourself, study hard, behave yourself, and learn. Help yourself and everybody will help you.

You say the little mule has gone crazy. Well, we have to treat him just the reverse of ordinary lunatics. Them you tie up. The little mule you must untie. So give him to Vangelo and tell Vangelo to take him to Montepugliano, and there remove his bridle and halter, and turn him loose, so that he can go where he wishes, earn his own living, and get over his craziness. There are big fields there. He is just a little mule. He can't possibly do any harm to anybody. Then, without worrying about him, we can see how he gets along. We can attend to catching him again when we are sure he has gotten his mind back.

Do with the other horses as Lodovico told you to do. I am glad he is well again and has sold the horses. I am sure that he has done well, since they were costing us money. But I am pained and angry that he has neglected to write.

Give my love to your mother, Marietta, and tell her that I have been on the point of leaving here from day to day, and so I am still. I have never been so eager to get back to Florence as I am now. Unfortunately, I can do nothing about it. Just tell her that she must be of good cheer whatever she may hear. I will be at home before anything serious happens.

A kiss to Baccina, to Piero and to Totto, if Totto is still there. I wish you had told me how his eyes are doing. So be cheerful, all of you, and spend as little as you can. Tell Bernardo to be careful to behave himself. Here I have written him twice in two weeks, and no answer! The Lord keep you all.

Niccolò Machiavelli in Imola

This brief death announcement, if it is authentic, confirms the impression that Machiavelli was a faithful servant of the State: like Cavour on his deathbed, "he allowed confession to be administered to him, respectful of everything that maintains the State." If the announcement is apocryphal, it represents a maneuver on the part of the Church to enroll an unbeliever among the number of true believers, and thereby takes on a wholly different meaning.

PIERO MACHIAVELLI TO FRANCESCO NELLO

Pisa, June 22, 1527

My dearest Francesco:

I can only weep as I have to tell you that Niccolò, our father, died here on this 22nd, of stomach pains caused by a medicine he took on the 20th. He allowed Brother Matteo, who was with him to the last, to hear his confession. Our father, as you know, left us in direst poverty. When you come back this way I shall have a great deal to tell you. Just now I am in a hurry and will say no more. My best compliments.

Your Relative Piero Machiavelli

SELECTED BIBLIOGRAPHY

I. STANDARD EDITIONS OF MACHIAVELLI'S WORKS IN ITALIAN

Mazzoni, Guido and Mario Casella (*eds.*). *Tutte le opere storiche e letterarie di Niccolò Machiavelli*. Firenze, G. Barbèra, 1929.

Bonfantini, Mario (*ed.*) *Opere di Niccolò Machiavelli*. Milano, R. Ricciardi, 1954.

II. EDITIONS OF MACHIAVELLI'S WORKS IN ENGLISH

The Discourses of Niccolò Machiavelli. Translated, with an introduction and notes, by Leslie J. Walker, S. J. New Haven, Yale University Press, 1950. 2 vols.

The Historical, Political, and Diplomatic Writings of Niccolò Machiavelli. Translated from the Italian by Christian E. Detmold. Boston, James R. Osgood and Company, 1882.

History of Florence. New York, Torchlight Books, 1961.

The Prince and The Discourses. With an introduction by Max Lerner. New York, Modern Library, 1950.

The Prince and Other Works including Reform in Florence, Castruccio Castracani, On Fortune, Letters, Ten Discourses on Livy. New translations, introductions, and notes by Allan H. Gilbert. New York, Hendricks House, Farrar, Straus, 1946.

Mandragola. New and complete translation by J. R. Hale. Oxford, Fantasy Press, 1956.

III. HISTORICAL AND POLITICAL BACKGROUND OF MACHIAVELLI'S THOUGHT

Burd, L. A. "Florence (II): Machiavelli" in *The Cambridge Modern History* (New York, The Macmillan Company, 1934), Vol. I, pp. 190-218.

Burckhardt, Jacob. "The State as a Work of Art," in *The Civilization of the Renaissance in Italy* (New York, The New American Library, 1960), Part I, pp. 39-119. (The translation of S. G. C. Middlemore, revised and edited by Irene Gordon; a Mentor book.)

Gilbert, Allan H. *Machiavelli's "Prince" and Its Forerunners*. Durham, North Carolina, University of North Carolina, 1938.

Roeder, Ralph. *The Man of the Renaissance*. New York, The Viking Press, 1933.

IV. STUDIES OF MACHIAVELLI IN ENGLISH

Acton, John Emerich Edward. "Introduction to L. A. Burd's edition of *Il Principe di Niccolò Machiavelli*" in Acton, *The History of Freedom and Other Essays*, edited by John N. Figgis and Reginald V. Laurence (London, Macmillan and Company, 1902), pp. 212-231.

Burnham, James. *The Machiavellians: Defenders of Freedom*. New York, The John Day Company, 1943.

Butterfield, H. *The Statecraft of Machiavelli*. London, G. Bell and Sons, Ltd., 1940.

Eliot, T. S. "Niccolò Machiavelli" in *For Launcelot Andrewes: Essays on Style and Order* (Garden City, N. Y., Doubleday, Doran and Company, 1929), pp. 47-65.

Laski, Harold. "Machiavelli and the Present Time" in *Dangers of Obedience and Other Essays* (New York, London, Harper and Brothers, 1930), pp. 238-263.

Lewis, Wyndham. *The Lion and the Fox*. London, G. Richards, Ltd., 1927.

Muir, D. Erskine. *Machiavelli and His Times*. London, W. Heinemann, Ltd., 1936.

Olschki, Leonardo. *Machiavelli as a Scientist*. Berkeley, Calif., The Gillick Press, 1945.

Praz, Mario. *Machiavelli and the Elizabethans*. London, The British Academy, 1928. (The annual Italian lecture of the British Academy, 1928.)

Prezzolini, Giuseppe. *Niccolò Machiavelli, the Florentine*. Translated from the Italian by Ralph Roeder. New York, Brentano's, 1928.

Pulver, Jeffrey. *Machiavelli: The Man, His Work, and His Times*. London, H. Joseph, Ltd., 1937.

Villari, Pasquale. *The Life and Times of Niccolò Machiavelli*. Translated by Madame Linda Villari. London, T. F. Unwin, 1892. 2 vols.

Note on bibliography: Achille Norsa's *Il principio della forza nel pensiero politico di Niccolò Machiavelli* (Milano, U. Hoepli, 1936) contains a 2143-item bibliography, pp. 1-248.

ACKNOWLEDGMENTS

Villari and Tommasini both agree that there is no authentic painting or sculpture of Machiavelli. But the Florentine engraving showing Machiavelli and the free Republic, which served as a model for a drawing by Jean Perraud, clearly dates from 1493.

Illustrations:

Giraudon, pp. 8a, c, 20, 116, 132, 159.
Alinari-Giraudon, pp. 25, 30, 33, 105c, d, 101, 114, 180.
Anderson-Giraudon, pp. 105a, 142.
Brogi-Giraudon, pp. 74, 75, 105f.
Alinari Florence, pp. 15, 47, 105e, 10.
Roger Viollet, pp. 8b, d, 16-17, 12, 90, 91, 105b, 4, 164.
Bibliothèque Nationale (Paris), pp. 6, 14, 44, 82, 87, 95, 117, 142.

Thanks are due for the following excerpts: From *The Living Thoughts of Machiavelli*, presented by Count Carlo Sforza, edited by Alfred O. Mendel; copyright 1940 by Longmans, Green and Co., copyright 1940 by David McKay Co., Inc.: David McKay Co. and Cassell and Co., Ltd. From *The Discourses of Niccolò Machiavelli*, tr. L. J. Walker: Routledge & Kegan Paul Ltd. From *The Private Correspondence of Niccolò Machiavelli*, tr. Orestes Ferrara: The Johns Hopkins Press. From *The Prince*, tr. Luigi Ricci, rev. E. R. P. Vincent: Oxford University Press. From *Mandragola*, tr. J. R. Hale: Fantasy Press, Oxford. From *The Prince and Other Works*, tr. Allan H. Gilbert: Hendricks House. The excerpts on pages 129-130, 138-139, 160-161, 173-174, 186, are new translations by Helen R. Lane. The translator wishes to acknowledge the work done on portions of the translation of this book by E. S. Seldon.